Also by Shepherd Mead

Tessie, the Hound of Channel One

The Magnificent MacInnes

HOW TO SUCCEED IN BUSINESS
WITHOUT REALLY TRYING

Shepherd Mead

With a New Introduction by Stanley Bing

SIMON & SCHUSTER PAPERBACKS
New York London Toronto Sydney

Simon & Schuster Paperbacks
A Division of Simon & Schuster, Inc.
1230 Avenue of the Americas
New York, NY 10020

Text copyright 1952 by Shepherd Mead
Copyright renewed © 1980 by Shepherd Mead
Introduction copyright © 2011 by Stanley Bing

First Simon & Schuster trade paperback edition January 2011

SIMON & SCHUSTER PAPERBACKS and colophon are registered
trademarks of Simon & Schuster, Inc.

For information about special discounts for bulk purchases,
please contact Simon & Schuster Special Sales at 1-866-506-1949
or business@simonandschuster.com

The Simon & Schuster Speakers Bureau can bring authors to your live event.
For more information or to book an event contact the Simon & Schuster Speakers
Bureau at 1-866-248-3049 or visit our website at www.simonspeakers.com

Manufactured in the United States of America

10   9   8   7   6   5   4   3   2   1

The Library of Congress has cataloged the Fireside edition as follows:

Mead, Shepherd.
    How to succeed in business without really trying / by Shepherd Mead. —
1st Fireside ed.
        p.   cm.
    "A Fireside book."
    1. Success in business.   2. Career development.   3. Management.
    HF5386.M48   1995
    650.1—dc20   94-48421
                                                                        CIP

ISBN 978-1-4516-2709-1

CONTENTS

Contents

HOW TO SUCCEED IN BUSINESS WITHOUT REALLY TRYING 2.0

BY STANLEY BING

You hold in your hands a groundbreaking object—the first book in more than 12,000 years of recorded workplace history to recognize that organized business is a very serious occupation that cannot for one moment be taken seriously. In this seminal work from the late corporate stone age, advertising executive and world-class wise guy Shepherd Mead put forth, in simple terms, the strategy by which anyone with a callow heart and certainly no more than half a brain can ascend to the heights of career success. Like Sartre, Camus, and many less amusing and readable philosophers before and after, Mead understood that the underlying truth of existence lies in its absurdity. He then set about turning that wisdom into fun and profit.

The resulting lean, luminous tome has spawned an enduring industry. Innumerable productions of the long-running, award-winning Broadway play that grew from this book have been enjoyed by generations of theatrically minded high school students and their poor parents. An excellent movie, too, tilled the ground initially turned over by the master, one that defined the reality of corporate life better than any other such effort, at least until Don Draper showed up with his fedora and vat of Canadian Club. All these offshoots, as well as the original, are built around a core premise still not recognized by all the squeaky, upbeat Dale Carnegie knockoffs or tedious B School scholars. And that phrase is this: Business is ridiculous.

People in business are, too. Only those who embrace the essential fatuity and irrationality of organizational life will survive and prosper. This was the first book that truly made these facts clear.

"If you have education, intelligence, and ability, so much the better," Mead advises the neophyte, then adds helpfully, "But remember that thousands have reached the top without them. You, too, can be among the lucky few." Thus he offers both an accurate assessment of the situation and an encouragement to the insecure among us. This is the way executives are, he tells us. They're a lot like you. Only richer, crazier, and lazier. But have hope. There is a way. And here it is.

And lo and behold, yes, here it is, chapter by minuscule little chapter, a yellow brick road made up of golden nuggets of hilarious stepping-stones. How to Delegate Responsibility. How to Write a Memo. How to Make More Money. One of the funniest things about his method is in fact how brief these chapters are, each dealing with subjects that occupy full shelves of your local chain bookstore, if any still exist, or could overload your iPad or Kindle without, you know, really trying. Most amazing is that, aside from some sociologically outré observations and dated terminology, very little of importance has changed since the days when Eisenhower was a brand-new Chief Executive.

I'll give you an example. In the chapter on How to Stop Being a Junior Executive, the author tells the story of how his hero, the archaically named Pierrepont Finch, succeeds in getting an office for himself by simply moving into one left vacant by somebody who was transferred, fired, or otherwise defenestrated. Then, relying on the amnesia of his bosses, he simply retains the purloined space until it somehow becomes his. Outlandish? You might think so. Except that is pretty much precisely how I received my first office.

True story: I arrived one morning at the corporation in order to write a speech for the CEO about something fictional he wanted to brag about even though we actually weren't doing it. When it was done, I was supposed to leave. Except I didn't. I just remained where I was, coming in every day and doing whatever people asked of me. The office I was in had been left empty during the most recent of the six dozen reorganizations that took place during that decade. After I had enjoyed about three months as a semi-temp, somebody from Human Resources found out about me and suggested I either be hired or be fired, limbo not being a status officially recognized by the seventeenth floor. Because I had possession of the office and was in the middle of some fatuous task or other, I got hired. And I kept the office, which was in fact a director-level office rather than the associate cubicle to which I was truly entitled. This also helped me get a fast promotion to director, by the way.

So when I read this little book, which purports to be humor, I don't view the stupid stuff Mead half kiddingly or ironically suggests as just funny or bizarre, although of course it is that. I also recognize what he's talking about as truth spoken in jest.

At the same time, like all works of human industry and spirit, this little book was and remains of its time. Many, many things have changed in the workplace since 1952. There is no booze, for instance. A guy who has a bar in his office and hits the hard stuff every morning at ten will be carted off to rehab, chop-chop. Also, you may not call a woman a girl. You could in 1952, I guess. Not now. You may not even call a secretary a secretary, any more than you can call a firefighter a fireman or a flight attendant a stewardess. You may not leave 99 cents' worth of flowers for your boss's executive administrative assistant, in hopes of getting on J.B.'s good side. This doesn't mean you don't need to manage her, even more than you do her boss, maybe. But the job is different. Likewise, if I were to use my computer to advise a young woman just out of business school to wear a sweater two sizes too tight, as Mr. Mead does at one point, I would draw nothing but a bloody stump away from my keyboard.

Operationally, things have changed as well. Except in very limited cases, mostly talent agencies, God help us, people don't start in the mailroom anymore. Some of Mead's early-career strategies must clearly be augmented, modulated, and slightly repositioned. And while his approach to memo writing is jammed with humor calories, if anybody fielded a six-page single-spaced paper memo to me now, copying nine people he wanted to impress? I would reposition his nose and then send him off to the field office in Petaluma. Today we do not have carbon paper. We have BlackBerrys and phones that are smarter than we are, and we are reachable even if we are hiding at the North Pole. And certain arts—like the art of sucking up or the manipulation of one's schedule—have changed profoundly in the years between then and now.

This is not a knock on the venerable Mead. We don't wear codpieces anymore, yet Shakespeare still speaks to us loud and clear. So for just a few moments, while we are still together, let's entertain a few thoughts on how the world has moved on and what, perhaps, we can do to make sure we continue to succeed. Since I'd like to do so without really trying, I'll steal some of his chapter headings.

How to Apply for the Job

Mead advised readers to work for a Big Corporation, one where vagueness of job description can hide a multitude of sins. While this is true, even big corporations have smaller and smaller departments nowadays, not to mention the fact that a lot of action takes place at tiny start-ups where everybody wears ripped T-shirts and calls each other dude. This healthy multiplicity of opportunity requires a different kind of style at times. The highly polished Brooks Brothers act may not suffice in all venues. So whatever you do, get on the Internet and learn a little bit about the company before you come in the door. Get in marginal tune with the corporate culture so that the interviewer can legitimately see you as a conceivable solution to the company's staffing problem. You can't gain entry to a grass-fed hipster cubicle farm in a cowboy hat and chaps, and "What do you guys do, anyway?" is not the answer to the interviewer's final polite query, "So, Bob, do *you* have any questions for me?"

The author also quite rightly stressed his conviction that it was bad to have any specific skill. He felt it limited your ability to be all things to all conceivable bosses and often tethered you to actual work, thus interfering with the indolence befitting a budding executive. I believe that while this is increasingly true as you climb up the ladder, it is often useful at the beginning of a career to be able to profess that you do something that has some temporal value. You're not an executive yet! The fact that you're the only one around there who can actually spell without Spell Check may turn out to be important. Don't hide your light under a bushel!

The Interview

Being a go-getter never goes out of style. The best way to ensure you do not get a job is to fail to specifically ask for it. You would be amazed how many people go in and talk like hiring them would do the corporation a big favor. This is a big attitudinal shift from the old days, when folks came in with a full vat of grease for the interviewer. Now people are cool. This is a bad idea for an interview. I've even had people who came late for an interview, then told me they were happy where they were and wanted to know what I could do for them. One of these guys was out of my office, at my request, in under three minutes. So I guess he did me a favor. I remember him too. That's saying something . . . although nothing very good.

Some things, however, have changed for the better, at least

insofar as the guy on my side of the desk is concerned. For reasons that are inexplicable to me, it seems that back in 1952, when Mead's Pierrepont Finch was clawing his way up the tree, people didn't always bring résumés to the interview. Mead has Ponty, as his friends were wont to call him, offer to send along his résumé if the interviewer was interested. Bizarre. Without a CV on hand, what does an interviewer talk about while feigning interest? World peace? Global climate change? Six Sigma? I know that if I can't ask the person about their junior year in Mozambique or their four miserable years at GE, I don't know what I'd do. Oh, and when it comes to résumés, please don't put your personal goals at the top or organize your personal info by some strange criteria, like skill set. One page, most recent job first. And don't lie about your prior salary. You will be busted.

How to Rise from the Mailroom

I don't know about your company, but in this day and age the line of succession doesn't begin in the bowels of the building. The only thing that's in the bowels is . . . well, what's usually in bowels. You don't want to start there, because that's where you're probably going to end. Nor does the beanstalk of greatness germinate behind the desk of a personal assistant except in the field of publishing, a business where achievement is measured in the high five figures and the guys at the top often do better when they're fired than they do when they actually get to keep their jobs.

I'm going to suggest a radical notion: If you're a young person just starting out, try to get a job in which you have some actual interest, one that could turn into a career. If you're looking for a crappy gig for lousy money, you can work at Chuck E. Cheese. There's no upside betting that medial will someday magically turn into genial. Start out by doing something where you can actually look at yourself in the mirror every morning. Or at least try. That way, when you do good, you just might get some career traction out of it, rather than being a very excellent mail handler or lunch reservation maker.

How to Stop Being a Junior Executive

Mead offers a host of excellent suggestions in this area which all add up to a strategy: Control your time, do the stuff you want to do, feign working harder than you actually are. Some of his suggestions are gratifyingly devious, involving guerrilla tactics like sleeping in the office to show how dedicated you are, even if you're not, or coming in on weekends when you know J.B. is dropping by to pick up his golf clubs.

Perhaps the most pointed suggestion—and one in need of amplification—involves the establishment of Places Other Than the Office at which you will be unreachable and incredibly busy. Pierrepont is often telling his boss that he'll be "at the plant" or "checking customer reactions" in the field and other bushwah like that. This was excellent during the days when people were legitimately unreachable a good part of the time. A guy could flake out for an entire day and nobody would be the wiser. Now we all might as well have ankle transponders. Everybody knows where everybody is, always. But don't despair. This is why God created the BlackBerry, the smart phone, and the road trip. Used in tandem, electronic communications and strategic travel can put you out of reach of boredom on a consistent basis.

The BlackBerry in particular is a fabulous tool for tooling around instead of working. It creates the impression of intense labor where none is in fact taking place. I know a guy who is almost always "in meetings" and has "just stepped away" during office hours, but is an absolute monster on the BlackBerry at all times of the night, on the weekends, and most impressively and consistently, on holidays. "Boy," people will say, "Larry is such a dedicated guy. Look at him forwarding tracking reports on Christmas morning!"

How to Delegate Responsibility

The capacity to make others do your work for you is the backbone of all management. Climbing up to the top, Pierrepont established the need for a group of assistants to do the work that he didn't want to do. As Mead observes, it creates the time necessary for a boss to do the real work of management: sitting and thinking.

It's tough these days to get assistants, however. They don't really exist, and if they do, you have to share them. It's much better to use junior associates who want to get exposure to YOUR bosses. They think that's a good thing, and sometimes it is. Let them go to the most boring meetings. Put their names on the cc list of e-mails they have generated for your signature. Give them profile. Then, of course, watch your back. The alternative to this policy of shifting labor from your shoulder onto others is really bad shoulder pain. That's worse than a little paranoia driven from below.

Mead also cleverly ascertains that there are three types of little people on whom you can foist your headaches: (1) grunts, (2) capable individuals with whom you will have to share some credit, and (3) superb performers who are just too ugly, illkempt, or misshapen for executive exposure. He favors the last, but lazy beggars can't be choosers. Like BlackBerrys and iPads, human tools are a necessity for Pierrepont, and for you.

How to Plan Your Day

I get a lump in my throat when Mead starts talking about how to manage your desk calendar. Remember those? Unless you're a geezer, probably not. They don't exist anymore, went out with Rolodexes. People who still use either, in my mind, wear bow ties and smell like baby powder.

How, then, should the savvy player establish that he or she is more busy than he actually is, thereby gaining access to one's own time with greater power and freedom? Simply by modernizing Pierrepont's strategy a bit, filling one's Outlook with notes, appointments, and inexplicable hooey, that's how. What is sometimes insufficiently noticed is that all assistants have access to their bosses' Outlook. They print them out when required. And they tell each other what's on them. "Oh, Jeff can't see Mr. Burbage then," Jeff's assistant will tell Mr. Burbage's. "He's got something from two to four, and from four-fifteen to six-thirty. Then he has drinks with somebody from Grey." Does Jeff really have all those things? Only Jeff knows! And right now Jeff is at the pool at the Four Seasons on Doheny, shooting out hostile messages from his BlackBerry that create work for other people!

The Meeting Is a Must!

Mead liked meetings and understood their mostly inane nature very well. He also saw them as opportunities for advancement, however, and advised he or she who wanted to succeed in business to go to a lot of meetings and cut a high profile. This may be good advice. It is certainly necessary, from an optical standpoint, to be in certain meetings; others should without question be delegated or, lacking the ability to do so formally, simply fobbed off. Never, of course, evade a meeting for which you are the fobbee. Only idiots and very powerful people may delegate stuff they've been delegated.

On the other hand, I personally have never been a big fan of junior folks piping up with a lot of random thoughts and opinions at open meetings with their older and stupider counterparts. I much favor quiet younger types, who look interested and have something cogent and brief to say when spoken to. And when it comes to advancement via meeting, I always found that the very best time was spent AFTER the gathering itself, when people were gathering up their papers and a short, smart word, joke, or observation could be made to Mr. Dithers. I once destabilized my then-boss, who was a real beast, by smart usage of post-meeting blather. You can too, I'm sure, as long as you're not working for me.

How to Write Memos

Books have been written on how to handle e-mail. Certainly some of the old wisdom on memos has been translated into current form, but the skill set is really quite different. Where memos could be long and full of pith, pith in e-mails is dangerous. Pith can be subpoenaed. I know a guy who wrote very funny e-mails to everybody over a long period of time. Then the company got sued. His deposition took twelve hours. It's really hard to explain jokes to a phalanx of hostile attorneys.

Likewise, the e-mail chain is the enemy of good management. You can really get to hate somebody who constantly tacks on an OK! or a THX or, worst, an emoticon, to an already bulbous e-mail chain. Brevity is the soul of wit. You have something more substantial to say? Use the damn phone.

Some Additional Thoughts

A lot has not changed, of course. People still steal each other's ideas, for instance, and the ones who are best at it rise to positions where they need not steal ideas anymore because they have all the good ones. People still bullshit each other about bogus research, which still tells the client exactly what he wants to hear. Sure, there are no more slide rules, which was the tool that Pierrepont used to cow his adversaries into silence. But there is jargon, which is most useful in making other people feel more stupid than they are. And in the end, as our guru makes very clear, it is all about the money. When people say "It's not about the money," you can be very sure that it well and most truly is. The job, then, is to always move forward, like a shark, eating small creatures as you go, ever moving forward and upward because the moment you stop doing that, your career dies, as do all the little remora who have attached themselves to you.

Good-bye and Good Luck

I have expended more time than I intended on this little introduction, and I have some serious sitting around and thinking to do, so I'll leave you to enjoy the real deal. I believe you'll agree, as you go along on this brief, merry ride, that while the outer shell of business may have changed over time, the beating heart of the matter has not.

Appearances are still all-important, particularly at the top.

Those who are armed with a strategy, no matter how insane or jejune, are better off than those who are not, who are destined to bounce around from one crisis to the next, being acted upon instead of acting.

And now, as in the past, it is very, very good to be the King or, as is increasingly common, the Queen.

Go forth. Have fun. Maybe in the end that's what Not Really Trying is all about.

AN INTRODUCTION

Hand in hand with our rules and little exercises we will include bits of illustrative dialogue. This is intended not to amuse but to clarify certain points.

All but a very few of these illustrative bits were taken *from life,* indeed from the very career of a man who was a living monument to the precepts of this work—and proof not only that our method *can* work, but that it *has* worked, and the evidence is there, for us all to see.

Our character has been dubbed Pierrepont Finch, though there will be few among you who won't break into a sly smile of recognition as his career is unfolded.

A WORD OF CAUTION!

This book will be beneficial only to those who bring to it purity of thought. It is designed *solely to show you how to succeed in business and to make money* and will be effective only to those who read it with these aims in mind. Those who bring with them selfish motives will receive small comfort and scant benefit.

HOW TO SUCCEED IN BUSINESS

WITHOUT REALLY TRYING

1

HOW TO APPLY FOR A JOB

L et us assume you are young, healthy, clear-eyed and eager, anxious to rise quickly and easily to the top of the business world.

You can!

If you have education, intelligence, and ability, so much the better. But remember that thousands have reached the top without them. You, too, can be among the lucky few.

Just have courage, and memorize the simple rules in the chapters that follow.

Choose the Right Company

This is the first essential, neglected by so many. There are thousands and thousands of "right" companies. Find them. Make sure *your* company fits these easy requirements:

1. *It must be BIG.* In fact, the bigger the better. It should be big enough so that nobody knows *exactly* what anyone else is doing.

2. *It should be in a Big City.* This is not essential, but it helps. New York City is best, but many others will qualify. The reasons are too complicated to be taken up here. (See "Be a Commuter" under "How to Plan Your Day," and "How to Play Company Politics.")

3. *Beware of "Service" Companies.* Be sure yours is a company that makes something, and that somebody else has to make it. Any company with a factory will do. Beware of organizations offering personal services, whether they be law of-

fices, advertising agencies, or animal hospitals. They will give you few opportunities to relax, or to plan your future.

This will leave you a wide field. Remember, you are about to embark on the sea of life. It is important to choose men you would like to *sail* with.

Don't Be a Specialist

If you have a special knack, such as drawing or writing, forget it. You may receive more at the very start for special abilities, but don't forget the Long Haul. You don't want to wind up behind a filing case drawing or writing!

It is the ability to Get Along, to Make Decisions, and to Get Contacts that will drive you ahead. Be an "all-around" man of no special ability and you will rise to the top.

How to Get the Interview

The first step is to get in, to get the appointment. A friend's recommendation is helpful, or a letter stating useful experience. But if you have no useful friends or any related experience, don't be discouraged!

Use an Idea. For Dad, a bright, chatty "come-on" letter and a snappy photo were enough. Not so today. Your prospect throws away a basketful of them every day. Your Presentation will have to stand out. Be original! Be dramatic!

Think how *you* would feel if you were a personnel man and a quartet arrived singing a clever set of lyrics like "He's a Big

Man, Rivers!" to the tune of "Old Man River." Or, "The Smith a Mighty Man Is He."

If your name isn't Rivers or Smith, a few moments' thought will turn up a dandy for *you*.

Another sock idea is a boxing glove and prayer book, attached to a snappy note beginning: "For that old Sunday punch you need a man like (INSERT YOUR NAME HERE).

Remember this: It's easy to drop a letter in the wastebasket, but it's hard to overlook a piece of artillery or a Shetland pony.

Think up one yourself. The surface has barely been scratched.

Warning: Avoid Sentimentality. A lock of your hair, a photo of you as a tiny tot, or a baby shoe may force a tear, but it will not get you a job.

References

Always include references in your presentation. If few people will speak well of you, list uncles or cousins with different surnames.

A good trick is to list a recently deceased tycoon, scratching his name off lightly.

> *"Poor Bunny," you will say later in the interview, "I'll take his name off my new résumé."*

Seize Your Opportunities

Though you, as a keen young man, must plot a straight course and an accurate one for your business career, leaving little to chance, you must nevertheless be ready on an instant's notice for the knock of Opportunity.

This is particularly true in the early stages before you make your connection.

Suppose, for example, you happen to run into the head of a large corporation:

> *"Oops, sorry, Mr. Biggley, didn't mean to knock you down!"*
> *"You blasted idiot!"*
> *"I was just coming to ask you for a job, sir—"*
> *"Dammit, you imbecile, what do you think we have a personnel man for?"*

Seize your opportunity! Go to the personnel man:

> *"I was speaking to J. B. Biggley only this morning."*
> *"Biggley himself?"*
> *"He said to see you."*
> *"Not old J.B.!"*
> *"Oh, yes. Just happened to run into him."*
> *"Well, well, Mr. uh—"*
> *"Finch. Pierrepont Finch."*
> *"Well, this may be over my level, Mr. Finch. Perhaps you ought to see Mr. Bratt."*

And so, in one way or another, you will have stormed the gates and the company of your choice will be quick to grant you that important interview.

2
THE INTERVIEW

Once you have been granted an appointment, prepare carefully.

How to Dress

The impression you must convey is that you don't really *need* this job—the job needs *you*. It is a challenge. Dress with this in mind.

The note is one of studied carelessness. By all means wear a Madison Avenue Sack Suit. If one is not available to you, borrow any old suit from a comparatively shapeless friend, remove the padding, and roll about in it on a clean level surface.

Accessories should be kept in the same minor key. A black knit tie is good for creating the feeling that you don't really give a damn. Wear shoes of the same pair. No good being *too* relaxed.

No Mustache

Avoid not only mustaches, but also sideburns and chin whiskers. Men with facial hair are seldom trusted. (Later you will have more latitude, as you will see in the chapter on Junior Executives.)

A Word to Women

Women are often hired by women, but it is well to be prepared for any emergency. If you're not sure of your interviewer, it is best to bring along a handy Convertible Kit. This consists of a Salvation Army hat (insignia removed), heavy glasses, zip-on Mother Hubbard, and an extra pair of flat-heeled shoes. These can all be slipped on quickly in the reception room after the receptionist says, "Miss Blank will see you now." If, of course, it is *Mister* Blank who will see you, just leave your equipment in a neat pile in the reception room. No one will take it.

Aside from your Convertible Kit dress carefully, with Mister Blank in mind. Nothing will be wasted because if you do get the job, these will be your regular working clothes.

It must be remembered that the well-bred girl is always fully clothed in the office. The broken shoulder strap, the deeply split skirt, and the bare midriff are *de trop* in most businesses. The bright girl soon learns that these devices are not only in bad taste, but are not necessary.

It is not skin area but *contour* that counts.

A few simple experiments with sweaters, jerseys, and a slightly smaller dress size will bring pleasing and surprising results. One young lady who made a careful study of contour planning found that results were little short of breathtaking. The male workers were stimulated and encouraged, and though production dropped slightly, it was *more* than made up for in better morale, and greatly improved esprit de corps.

A common stumbling block to contour planning is occasional lack of contour. However, those not blessed by nature need not be discouraged. Science has come to your rescue! Several good commercial devices may now be purchased freely.

The fact that your contour-corrected attire may seem sexy should not disturb you. Sex will be farthest from the male interviewer's thoughts! He will be thinking of your mind. However, he will have learned in the School of Hard Knocks that good minds are most often found in good bodies, and that beauty and brains only too often go hand in hand!

The Casual Manner

Always remember that in business there are plenty of grubby little people to do the work, but a person of real charm is a pearl indeed. This is what your interviewer will be seeking and you must help him (or her) to find it.

Remain relaxed, casual, friendly, and sympathetic. Imply that you, too, have sat on his side of the desk.

> *"I know what a nasty chore this interviewing is,"* you say.
> *"You get used to it."*
> *"I wouldn't mind if it were always* people like us.*"*

Note the "people like us." It is always well to *include the interviewer*.

Some other valuable phrases:

> *"The money is secondary. I'd like to be one of you people."*

Or:

"The human values are the important thing, don't you think?"

Don't Be Pinned Down

He will be interested in you *as a person*. Encourage this. But he may ask you specific questions about experience, just to make conversation. Parry these skillfully.

"But exactly what did you do, *Mr. Finch?" he may ask.*
"All phases of the operation. I'll send you a detailed résumé." (He'll forget this.)
"But couldn't you tell me just one—"
"I like that picture! Van Gogh?"

Keep him off balance. But keep things on a high plane!

"Why Did You Leave?"

If you are leaving a job, or if you have a job and are seeking a better one, you may be asked, "Why did you leave?" or "Why do you want to leave?"

Even if you were fired, and thrown bodily out the door, remember this: *Don't be bitter.* This would mark you as a sorehead or difficult personality.

Remember these phrases:

"They're a grand bunch of people."

Or:

"They were mighty happy years, mighty."

Since this, of course, will not answer your interviewer's question, he may repeat, "Well, then, why did (do) you want to leave?"

Tread carefully here! The impression you want to convey is that you can get along with *anyone,* no matter how difficult. Imply that you, somehow, were *above* them.

"I felt that I had outgrown them," is useful.

Or:

"Let's face it. They're not up to you *people."*

Or:

"Well, it's *an* old *outfit. I want to work with* young *men."*
(If the interviewer is young.)

Or (if he is old):

"Somehow they seem a bit callow. I want a shop with experience!*"

After a few such interviews you will be hired quickly. You will then have your foot on the first rung of the ladder.

3

HOW TO RISE FROM THE MAILROOM

[NOTE: Those who have already risen from mailrooms, or managed to bypass them altogether, need not learn this chapter by heart. It will be enough to run through it quickly a few times, jotting down important points. These may help you to rise from other things.]

Beginners often spend their first golden months—or years—in the mailroom or shipping department. Years hence, when you are careworn, harried, and tax-ridden, you'll look back fondly on those golden, carefree times and see yourself as you were then, clad only in a three-button West-of-England tweed, cheeks tanned, eyes clear, trudging happily to the post office with a sack of mail.

But remember, the thing is to Get On, to succeed, to escape from the mailroom, and it is to this purpose that this chapter is written. Let us leave the nostalgia to other, more skillful pens.

How to Dress

After you have made your mark you may cultivate a studied carelessness, but the mailroom man must always make a good impression. In fact, it is impossible for an ambitious young apprentice to be *too* well dressed.

Dress at all times as though you were attending an informal wedding or tea dance: conservative—but well-cut—lounge suit, the best white linen, carefully knotted four-in-hand from

Sulka or Countess Mara, and good, well-boned boots. Do not be concerned with expense.

How to Live

How, indeed, the fainthearted will cry, if your tailoring bills alone more than consume your $27.50 a week? Never fear. If you are one of those poor devils without independent income or generous women friends, you can still survive easily. Supper money and judicious use of "taxi" money will allow you to eat lightly.

You need not pay rent. You will find that the offices of your firm's executives are handsomely equipped and comfortable. They are, in addition, often in a fashionable part of town and are, of course, close to your work. Choose an office with a large comfortable couch and quiet exposure. Some prefer one facing east. It is cheerful to see the sun rise! Generally speaking, the higher the executive the larger the office, the more comfortable the couch, and the later he will come in mornings. As long as you are out by nine-fifteen, no one will complain.

You need not perform menial tasks. It is extravagant to wear out a pair of $30 brogues on a simple errand! Keep the phone number of a good messenger service at your fingertips. While the fellow is delivering his package, wait at your university club, using the time profitably to plan your promotion.

Some Useful Tips on How to Be Promoted

1. *Attract Attention.* Let them know you're there—in a well-bred way, of course.

After an especially difficult assignment return with package directly to executive's office (not to the mailroom!) with visible evidence of hardship. A bit of blood is helpful, if wiped from the face in a devil-may-care manner as you enter his office.

> *"You must have gone through hell, boy!"* he will say.
> *"Finch, sir, Pierrepont Finch."* (Always be careful to establish the name.) *"It was nothing, sir."*
> *"Blood, eh?"*
> *"Just a scratch. Some hoodlums tried to take it from me."*
> *"Oh?"*
> *"Taught* them *a lesson, sir!"*

But don't *push!* Remember, the elevator and the men's room are the only places where you will meet the executives on a man-to-man basis. Don't press your advantage. Just a word or two is enough.

> *"Damned fine memo of yours on the wicket situation, sir,"* you will say.
> *"Oh, you like it, uh—"*
> *"Finch, sir. I agreed with almost all your recommendations."* (Note the "almost.")

2. *Read Memos.* You will soon find there is little information of any value in them (see chapter on Memos, How to Write), but they are mighty handy in cases like the above.

3. *Write Memos.* Write them on any subject. Small matter what you write them *about,* as long as you write them often. No one will read them, but someone will notice your name at the top.

4. *Two Heads Are Better Than One.* The chap who uses his head will not long stay in the mailroom. Ideas are the thing, but you may find that because of your boyish appearance and young open face few people will take you seriously.

Don't be disheartened! Remember that two heads are better than one, especially if the other one belongs to an influential executive.

A quick run through the files will turn up a number of ideas over which some of the executives have fought long losing battles.

Read all the correspondence on one of these, then approach the man whose baby it was:

> *"Oh, pardon me, sir, I know it's presumptuous of me, but I haven't been able to sleep lately for thinking of the wicket retreading situation."*
>
> *"Yes? Well, come in, son!"*
>
> (At the very words "wicket retreading" he will begin to breathe more rapidly.)
>
> *"Finch, sir, Pierrepont Finch. Please tell me if I'm on the right track."*

Then rehash his whole idea in your own words.

> *"Well, what do you think, sir?"*
>
> *"I think it'll work, Finch! I know it'll work. And it would have worked, too, except for an, uh, political situation."*
>
> *"You mean it isn't a new idea?"*
>
> *"You couldn't know that, son. Before your time. Incredible, though, boy of your age. Miss Willoughby, will you bring in that wicket retreading file—'48 I believe—and don't disturb us. I'd like to spend some time with this boy. Yes, uh—"*
>
> *"Finch, sir."*
>
> *"Yes, Finch, you must have a mighty good head on your shoulders!"*

From this point on he will consider you his protégé. You will be sure to have the first vacancy in his department.

This technique is far easier than thinking up your own ideas—and far more effective.

5. *Be Generous with Your "Buddies."* The lad marked for success is one who is openhearted and unselfish, happy to share his good fortune with others, particularly his colleagues of the mailroom.

The callow chaps around you may not look like much, but they may well be tomorrow's captains of industry. Make them your "buddies." These rough-and-ready friendships will stand you in good stead in the years to come.

For example, suppose the personnel manager calls you into his office and says:

"Oh, Finch, we've been keeping an eye on you!"

"You have, sir?"

(It is well to be noncommittal at this stage.)

"Yes, you may not realize it, but we keep a mighty close watch over all you fellows. I think you may have the stuff, Finch."

"Thank you, sir."

"In fact, we've decided to give you a nice promotion. You've done so well as a mail boy that we're thinking seriously about putting you in charge of the whole mailroom!"

At this point the run-of-the-mill fellow would accept willingly. Not you! Remember, be generous! Be *big!* Look him straight in the eye and say:

"Decent of you, sir, damned decent! And you know how I'd like to accept. Don't see how I can, though, in all honesty."

(He will look at you with new interest.)

"No?"

"Don't really deserve it, sir. Watson is your man. Quiet chap, not one to attract notice, but he's earned that job!"

Be sure you tell Watson what you've done for him. He'll be your friend for life, and of course he'll still be in the mailroom, running it efficiently, long after you have gone ahead to higher things. (The personnel man won't forget how big you were about this!) It will pay off in extra service, too.

"Oh, Watson, send a boy up to my place, will you? These pencils are getting frightfully dull."

"Can't spare one, but I'll come myself for you, Ponty."
"That's a good boy, and make it quickly, will you?"

Of course, if the first offer of promotion will take you *out* of the mailroom it is better to accept.

No good being *too* generous!

Just follow these simple rules for a few months and you will quickly be summoned to the department of your choice.

"Finch, we feel you're our type of man! We're taking you into the department. You'll sit at the old desk in back of the mimeograph machine. Only temporary, of course. And you'll get more money, too. Think I can swing $2.50 more a week!"

This is what you have worked for! You're a Junior Executive. No one can stop you now!

4

HOW TO STOP BEING
A JUNIOR EXECUTIVE

A junior executive is any male in an office who sits down.

At first you will make considerably less money than the men who run the elevators, wash the windows, and shine the shoes. But remember—you are being paid not in money but in experience. You are learning! Some men spend their whole lives doing this, and when they finish they may have little in the bank, but they are rich indeed.

However, you are headed for the Top, so don't overdo this. Learn the business, yes, but you have other far more important things to learn, too.

Your Mission

As a Junior Executive you are the very pillar on which modern business rests.

It is you who must shoulder the load while Top Management *thinks*. Yes, this is what they are doing, thinking. They may not look it, but they are.

It will be your job, as a Junior Executive, to take over as many of their worries as you can. This will leave them as little as possible to think about.

Your Appearance

The keynote now is one of maturity, and of cheerful suffering.

Clothes. You need buy few clothes, since the Junior Executive does not dress as elegantly as the mailroom boy. Simply have your brighter, more dashing items dyed mouse color or Oxford gray, and sprinkle lightly with dandruff.

Look Older. But don't be too obvious about it! Do not wear high-button shoes, green eyeshades, or sleeve protectors.

Never exaggerate the importance of a few gray hairs, especially in the temples. This will mark you as a man of judgment. There are a number of good commercial preparations which are inexpensive and easy to apply.

Mustache. A mustache, well cultivated and closely cropped, will add years and a look of sly cunning. This latter, though undesirable as we have seen in job applicants, is a real Plus in the Junior Executive.

The Look of Suffering. The Junior Executive is expected to suffer, and if you cannot manage it, you must at least *appear* to. An ulcer is excellent. Grow one if you can, but if you cannot, a bottle of milk placed conspicuously on the desk will do nicely, if accompanied by a slightly pained smile.

Your Office Is Important

The caste of a Junior Executive is determined by the size and magnificence of his office. In fact, when your office is indistinguishable from that of the Senior Executives you will *be* a Senior Executive.

Your first step will be to get *any* office. Few will listen to a man who sits at a hall desk. When you see an opportunity, go quickly to the office manager:

> *"I see that Mr. Grabble is leaving, sir."*
> *"That's right."*
> *"Do you mind if I move my things in there until the new man comes?"* (Note: Never say "have the office!" It is always: "move my things in.")
> *"Is there a new man?"* (There isn't.)
> *"Hadn't you heard? Should be in any day now."*

You will be allowed to "move your things in" temporarily. After a few months everyone will forget it isn't your office and it *will* be.

The Head Cold Approach is equally successful:

> *"Frideful code in the head,"* you say to the *Office Manager, sneezing violently.*
> *"Oh, too bad, Finch."*
> *"Wonder if I could sid in the ebty office for a few days. Draft out here is derrible."*
> *"Well, for a few days I think it'll be all right."*

Such a cold can hang on for weeks. By this time it is wise to administer the coup de grâce:

> *"I don't like to cobplain, but my office is fridefully drafty."*
> (Note "my office.")

"Oh?"

"The one in the corner seebs to get the sun. This code, you know. Maybe you could swidge O'Brien in here. Strong as an oggs, O'Brien."

"We'll see what we can do, Mr. Finch."

After the transfer, the office will be yours until it no longer suits you.

Continue the process until you have at least four windows. A four-window man is one to be reckoned with!

The Furnishings. It is a careless man who neglects these! You will have to decide first what mood you want to create. Some prefer the severe and monastic, with straight chair and table instead of swivel chair and desk; others favor soft lights, oriental rugs, and incense; others, rococo; and still others, the tooled leather and old gold nothing-is-too-good-for-me approach.

Decide for yourself. Fit your personality. Your office is a frame for *you!*

In most cases you will want a generous supply of sofas, easy chairs, portable bars, credenzas, and bric-a-brac. The company will supply these.

But remember that a caste system governs all office furnishings as well as offices. Furnishings are handed down until— by the time they reach the Junior Executive—they are a sorry sight indeed. It is simple to beat this unfair system, if you remember the *Magic Time.*

There is a Magic Time to pick up really suitable furnishings.

First, prepare a list of the different items you would like, in various offices. Then, as their occupants leave the company or are transferred, simply summon the porter:

"Oh, John, sometime today will you pick up that break-front in Crabtree's old office?"

"I thought the new man was coming in Thursday, Mr. Finch."

"He is. Crabtree wanted me to have the breakfront, though. He mentioned it specially. When you bring it in, move it against this wall, please, next to the bar. You can take this old thing here and move it in for the new man. He may like it, you know."

Soon you will have a real showplace.
But always remember—you are not doing this for yourself.

"It's quiet," you will say, "that's the important thing. These six windows are a distraction, but I don't really mind. Just give me a desk, a pencil, and a piece of paper. I can work anywhere."

Desk Management

You will soon have to decide whether to adopt the very full or very empty desk approach. There is no middle ground. A few papers on a desk look messy and inefficient. The keen young man keeps either a polished expanse of bright wood or a great overflowing mass of work. The one indicates cleanliness and efficiency, the other herculean effort and overwork.

Both are good. Decide now which course you will follow.

Calendar Management

The same reasoning applies to the notations on your desk calendar, which is on top of your desk, for all to see. Confine yourself to one or two simple notations, such as:

> *"J. B.—All Day.*
> *Lunch—Stork. B. S."*

The "Lunch, Stork"—"Lunch, Colony"—or "Lunch, 21" is advisable in all cases, even if you plan to duck out for franks and beans at a lunch counter.

Or, you may prefer the Cluttered Calendar approach, with dozens of appointments, scores of notations, appointments scratched out and replaced with others. This is especially effective if combined with the absolutely clean desk. It creates an impression of feverish but antiseptic activity—and will win you admiration everywhere.

5

HOW TO DELEGATE
RESPONSIBILITY

Your task as a Junior Executive will be to assume responsibility, to take cares and worries on your powerful young shoulders, and remove them from older, grayer heads.

The more responsibility you can assume, the better. Some useful phrases are:

"Why not just roll it all into one ball of wax, J.B.?"

Or:

"The whole thing needs to be buttoned up."

However, keep in mind that your real function is Formulating Policy and Making Decisions, the work for which you were chosen, and work which is best done in a relaxed, semi-reclining position.

Therefore, your first duty on assuming extra responsibility is to find capable assistants who will do the actual routine work.

The first step, of course, is to select the right secretary.

Hand-Pick Your Secretary

By the time you have reached a position of real responsibility you will probably be in the one-window stage, and will be able to say good-bye forever to the steno pool.

You are ready to have your own private secretary. Choose her carefully! Many a rising young man has been broken by careless or frivolous choice of secretaries. A Secretary is NOT a Toy. She will be a girl selected for her ability, at one thing or another, and she will only too often be skillful with the typewriter, and perhaps even shorthand. She will be entrusted to your care as a helpmate *in your work,* and should not be used for pleasure, except in emergencies.

Does She Belong to Another? If the young lady assigned to you is so attractive that you feel things are too good to be true, tread carefully.

Ask yourself this question: Does she belong to another?

It may be that one of the really big men in the company has become Interested-in-Her-Career, and has given her to you as a secretary. He will want to be sure she is kept busy during the day. Keep her busy! But keep your distance.

If your flesh is weak, avoid temptation. Help her to rise to the top. You, too, can rise with her. Approach your immediate superior, the man whose niche you feel destined to fill, and say:

"Oh, Mr. Gatch, I hardly know how to say this, but Hedy just happened to remark how much she admired you."

"Oh, did she, Finch? She's quite a girl, all right, quite a girl!"

"She was wondering whether you, uh, might be interested in having her work for you."

"Frankly, Finch, I'd love it, but I kind of suspected that old J.B. might, well, you know—"

"Nothing to it, Mr. Gatch! Broke up months ago—if it existed at all!"

(Note: Little white lies like this are to be encouraged if your intentions are good.)

She will be grateful to you, and when, after a short time, your superior is fired, you will be moved in quickly to fill his shoes.

Do not be too hasty about advancing the young lady to the next man ahead of you. It is well to wait until the dust settles and tempers cool.

Go to Extremes. The wise young businessman practices moderation in most things. However, this is not true in the choice of secretaries. Go all out. Take no halfway measures.

You must decide for yourself which choice you will make, the beauty or the beast.

The Beauty. If you decide on this course, select a girl of ravishing beauty, first making sure she does not belong to another.

Soon your little corner will become a mecca for influential men.

"Thought I'd drop around and see what Finch thinks about it."

"Finch? He in on this?"

"Well, not exactly. Good head on the boy, though. Real pleasure to be around him."

You will make many valuable and lasting friendships.

If the young lady looks to you for comfort and guidance, be

generous. Supply it. Emotion and sentiment have their places, even in the workaday world.

The Beast. Some prefer to take the opposite tack. Select the oldest, fattest, and least attractive woman in the building. Leave no stone unturned. With thirty or forty years experience in the company, she will be able to do all your dull, routine work better than you can. This will leave you free to think, decide, and endear yourself to those around you.

And she will give you an immediate and enviable reputation.

> *"Solid citizen, that boy Finch!"*
> *"Oh?"*
> *"Well, I mean, just look at his secretary! No fooling about* that *boy!"*

And you'll have no worries about her getting married, having babies, or other nonsense. She'll be yours for keeps.

Have Plenty of Assistants

You cannot have too many able helpers! If the management is balky at first, it will be your duty to educate and indoctrinate.

> *"As I see it, J.B.,"* you begin, *"the job breaks down like this. I drew up a little chart."*
> (Organizational charts filled with little lines and rectangles are valuable here.)
> *"Oh?"*
> *"Now we'll need three more men—A, B, and C, here."*

"Three more men? I thought you were going to do the—"

"I'll hold the reins of course. Have a pretty clear idea who the men should be, too!"

The Work Demonstration. If the above doesn't succeed, you may be forced to put on a Work Demonstration.

For two or three days and nights—two should be ample—remain in the office, consuming nothing but black coffee and cigarettes. Send your secretary around occasionally to borrow benzedrine tablets. Do not change clothes, but have a barber come in daily to shave you—*while you dictate.*

On the morning of the third (or fourth) day, walk cheerfully in to your superior's office.

"Lord!" he will say. *"You're looking frightful, Finch!"* (You will be.)

"It's nothing, J.B. Feel like a million."

(Assume an overhearty expression.)

"You were absolutely right about the assistants, J.B. Think I can carry on alone. Four or five months more like this and I'll have the whole thing whipped into shape."

At this point sink slowly to the floor with a brave smile, and twitch for a few seconds. Then lie still, eyes closed. Maintain just the trace of a smile!

You will be sent on a long vacation, and will return to find your assistants, ready for your instructions.

By this time you will surely be On Your Way. But we have not yet—as you will see—really scratched the surface.

6
HOW TO PLAN YOUR DAY

It must always be remembered that hard work is the very lifeblood of modern business. You, too, must be ready to pull your share of the load. This may call for personal sacrifices on your part—but no matter—your work should come first.

Know Your Own Breaking Point

Willing as you may be to dedicate your life to your business, remember that you will be of small value to your company if you reach the breaking point.

Know your limitations, and stay within them!

After-Hour Management

The conscientious businessman will make every moment count, and the moments that count most are those spent *after regular business hours.*

If you manage after-hour planning skillfully, you can achieve pleasing and surprising results and also free your mind for truly High Level thinking, which is your major function.

Remember, the hours you are assumed to be at work, the regular office hours, are of little value. The hurly-burly of office routine will interfere with long-range thinking.

Any good after-hour planner can find ample reason to be away from his desk from nine to five on week days. At nine-thirty, remark:

"Oh, J.B., anything you want from me before I take off?"

"Going out, Finch?"

"Yes, sir. Don't trust that survey at all. Think I'll get out and ring some doorbells. Got to get down to the grass roots, you know."

"Good boy, Finch."

You may then proceed to any calm, restful spot. A day out in the open will stimulate your brain. When you return to the office in a day or two, your mind will be clear, and bursting with ideas.

Some alternate approaches are:

"Want to get out and check the stores. Got to see if we're really moving off the shelves."

Or:

"Think I'll run out to the plant. Quality check, you know."

But the after-hour planner will be careful to be in the office after hours *at the right times!*

If you hear, for example, that the boss is going to drop in to the office Saturday morning, if only to pick up his golf clubs, be there a half hour ahead of him.

Roll up your sleeves, tousle your hair, and loosen your collar. Several empty paper coffee cartons and a few hundred cigarette butts will also help. (The cartons and butts can be kept in a drawer and used again.)

You will be noticed!

"Oh, working this morning, Finch?"

"Mmmmmmm. Is it morning already, sir?"

"Great Scott, been here all night?"

"No, not all *night! Just trying to clean up a few things. Shouldn't be here much longer."*

(Avoid any hint of self-pity!)

"Oh, that's good."

"Is there any way I can get in tomorrow, sir? Just in case. The night watchman is very fussy."

After the boss goes, wait ten or fifteen minutes and leave. It will not be necessary to come in Monday. Never fear; your employer will defend you hotly.

"Finch isn't in again today, sir!"

"I should think not! Poor devil worked all weekend! I ought to know. I was in here with him, working side by side!"

(You may count on the wise employer's knowing his after-hour techniques, too! He will be Setting a Good Example.)

"Too bad," he may continue, *"that there aren't more men like Finch around here!"*

Be a Commuter

Another way to conserve your strength is to establish early that you are a commuter, and that you have a frightful problem with trains.

If, for example, you have to lie abed late, wrestling with a knotty problem, you need only say:

> *"Damned Long Island Rail Road!"*
> *"Oh, train late again, Finch?"*
> *"Almost two hours."*
> *"Funny. Mine was on time."*
> *"But we're on the spur, you know. Always a bottleneck."*

The same approach may be used in the evening.

> *"Have to run, J.B."*
> *"Now? It's only three-thirty!"*
> *"Trestle. Blazing like hell this morning. Lucky if I get home at all."*

It is not necessary to *be* a commuter, as long as everybody *thinks* you are one. A chap who had bachelor's quarters three blocks from the office left regularly every day at 4:38 on the dot.

> *"Have to, you know. Got to get the 5:01. Next train doesn't come till eight!"*

"Poor devil. Well, see you tomorrow!"

"May be late, though. Damned thing doesn't get in till 10:17!"

He avoided strain and overwork, and by devoting his extra time to clear thinking, rose rapidly to the top.

The more obscure and mysterious your form of transportation, the better. Fictitious railroad lines are good, if the names are well chosen. Some recommendations: South Jersey Central; Newark, Hackensack, and Quogue; New York, Hartford, and Providence. One expert maintained for years that he lived on "the Putney Division," commenting only:

"Nothing like that ride through the mountains every morning. Never seems like three hours!"

Some helpful phrases:

"Third rail, you know. Ice."

Or:

"Did the last twelve miles by bus!"

You will no doubt find other and perhaps better ways to conserve your strength.

7
THE MEETING IS A MUST!

The farmer spends his time in the fields, the laborer at his machine, and the businessman at meetings.

You may feel at first that the meeting is a waste of time, a useless expenditure of energy, accomplishing little. Nothing could be farther from the truth!

A meeting is a Sounding Board, a Confluence of the Minds, a means of preventing junior executives from hiding their lights under a bushel.

The object of a meeting is not, as the very young believe, to solve the problem at hand, but to impress the people there. And for this purpose, of course, the larger the meeting the better.

If you are new to business, you have small inkling of the happy hours that lie ahead, the little glows of triumph, the camaraderie, and the tingling, heady sensation of hearing your own voice!

But these rich wines are not to be gulped willy-nilly. There are many bitter lessons to learn. Study carefully the following outline of the strategy and tactics of meetings.

1. *Never Be at a Loss for Words.* If you cannot give a ringing, extemporaneous speech—and so few can—it is wise to prepare a series of little talks, complete with gestures and a few jolly anecdotes, that will fit the subject of any meeting. Some suggested topics:

"We've all got to Pull Together on this!"

Or:

"We'll lick them at their own game, damn it!"

Other dandy ones will come to you.

2. *Be Decisive.* Your own mind must always be clear, and made up, whether or not you understand what everybody is talking about. *Leave the shilly-shallying to others.* Yours must be the steady hand to which others turn.

3. *But Avoid a Decision.* There is an anticlimactic, soggy feeling about a meeting after a decision has been reached. There is little danger of this, as we will see, but don't relax. You will know that the little problem at hand is only the *excuse* for the meeting. Yet to some, your remarks—inspiring as they may be—will have a hollow ring if delivered after the decision.

Follow this easy method, if a meeting is in danger of ending:

"Well, that seems to button up the matter, eh Finch?"
"Really? I don't get any nourishment out of that at all! Let's re-examine!"

(You can always re-examine.)

4. *The Sleeper Play.* Never speak first. Let the others talk themselves out. Then come slowly into action:

"As I sit here and listen to all of you, it seems to me that there's one basic fallacy to all your reasoning."

(At this point, go ahead and say what you had planned to say in the first place. It is not necessary to have listened, except in a general way, to what has gone before.)

5. *The "If George Were Only Here" Device.* If someone opposes you, try to have the meeting when he is out of town. Then preface your remarks with: "If George were only here I'm sure he'd agree that—" Proceed then to demolish George's entire position.

6. *The All-Out Attack, or Sweeping the Meeting Off Its Feet.* Effective, yes, and exhilarating, too! Some prefer simple shouting or table pounding, but the true virtuoso can cry, roll on the floor, stand on furniture, remove clothing, gag, spit, and use flip cards and slide films. All these have their places.

7. *Underplay.* A good variation of the above is the reverse twist. You can create a crushing effect by underplaying. Assume a wounded expression, and say in a tiny, hurt voice:

"Why do you do *this to me?"*

This is most effective if you have previously terrorized the meeting, or if you have a reputation for unusual ruthlessness.

8. *The Filibuster.* This is of value only if an opponent has to make a train or see a customer or client. Read a file of fifty or sixty letters, more or less related to the subject.

9. *Be a Meeting-Leaver.* The true Meeting-Leaver rarely attends meetings—he just leaves them. This is good. It places you somehow *above* the meeting you're leaving, and implies that you're going to another that is more important.

> *"Wish I could stay longer with you fellows. Another meeting, you know—"*

At the other meeting (and there is *always* another meeting somewhere) you say the same thing—but *do not return to the first meeting.* Remember this. *Never go back!*

10. *Beware the Do-It-Now-er!* At every meeting there will be some crude fellow who does not understand the true purpose of the Meeting as a Forum and Sounding Board. He will always try to "get something done." He may open a meeting like this:

> *"Well, fellows, this is something we really should be able to decide in five minutes. I just want a quick reaction."*

He will soon find himself without friends—and perhaps without employment.

Occasionally something *will* have to be decided. The decision will be made by the one really in authority, who wouldn't have attended the meeting anyway.

> *"Well, Finch, what did you boys decide?"*

"Uh, we didn't quite resolve it, J.B. But it was a good *meeting."* (Meetings are always "good" meetings.) *"I think we all see the problem clearly. I presented my case about buying, both pro and con."*

"Mostly pro, I hope. I bought it this morning."

8
HOW TO WRITE MEMOS

You will soon learn that the heart, the very lifeblood of modern business is the interoffice memo. If you're a good man with a memo you have small cause to worry.

The memo, like the meeting, is concerned only incidentally with its apparent subject. The main object of the memo is to *impress the people who read it.*

Never Come Straight to the Point

The neophyte can be spotted quickly. He comes right out and states his business. Since very few problems can't be covered in a paragraph or two, the reader is finished with it rapidly, and the whole point of the memo is lost.

A good man can expand the simplest subject into three or four closely written pages, during the course of which he can inject sympathetic understanding, wit, and a few well-chosen anecdotes. Those who read it will see that he not only has a complete grasp of the subject, and of the entire industry, but that he is a capital fellow, and is somehow slightly above the whole thing.

How to Get People to Read Memos

Memos are like seeds in the forest or the eggs of a salmon. The waste is staggering. One authority feels that if one in ten falls on target, or is at least partly read, the mission is accomplished. Another feels that one in twenty-five is a fair average. This is defeatist thinking! Make sure *your* memos are read. Address them to the highest officer who might be even remotely connected with the subject, especially the man who is in charge of those you are trying to impress. This name is usually referred to as "nominal sendee," or "reader guarantee." Address it:

To: Mr. Biggley
From: Pierrepont Finch   cc.

Under "cc.," or "carbon copy," list all those you're trying to impress.

This will make some of the carbon copy people read it on the chance that Biggley *might* read it and refer to it.

It is, of course, unnecessary to send out Biggley's copy.

The Secondary Target

The secondary target is the person who really has to do something about the memo, if he can find the right paragraph. This fellow, probably in some menial job, will receive the ninth carbon, which is not readable, except in a general way. It is sufficient to call him up:

"Say, don't know whether my memo got there yet."
"Oh, yessir, it did, Mr. Finch. Little trouble reading it."
"Well, don't bother. I can tell you in a nutshell. J.B. called from the agency and wanted to make sure you ship out a case to Akron."

"Oh, yes. I will."
"Fine."

The subtleties, the sly humor, and the gentle wisdom of your five closely written pages will have been lost upon this dolt, but no matter. Your purpose has been achieved.

Don't Pin People Down

It is not considered cricket to pin people down to specific details in a memo. If you ask a colleague if he has "seen" your memo and he answers yes, accept the statement. Those who ask what he thought of paragraph three will soon have few friends.

What to Do with Other People's Memos

There are two schools of thought on this. One holds that it's enough to place a bold red check on the upper right-hand corner. This shows your secretary you have "seen" it. She will then place it in a neat pile until you "have time to read it." This, of course, will never be necessary. Instruct her to throw away all memos six inches below the top of her pile.

The other procedure is to take freshly received memos, and, before reading, return to sender with a penciled note at the top. "Mighty clear exposition!" is always good, or "See you've really thought this through!" This way *is* more trouble, but it will make you friends.

If there is anything you really have to *do* about a memo, have no fear! The sender will phone you, as noted above.

Sample Memo

Excerpts from a sample memo are printed here, almost exactly as they appeared in Finch's personal file. No need to add that names—and an occasional fact—have been changed.

Study this carefully. It is a fine example of the memowright's art, coming as it does in the middle of Finch's early, or bold, period. But do not try to imitate it too slavishly. Remember that a memo is *you,* and one that may express another's personality will do you scant justice.

Memo
To: Mr. J. B. Biggley   Date:

The copy to J. B. Biggley, the "nominal sendee," was not sent, as explained above.

cc. Messrs.	Axel	
	E. Biggley	D. Osterly
	Cottery	Sprockett
	Fribble	Taffle
	Lightly	Womper

The above names are "impressees," or those the sender was trying to impress. They are always listed in alphabetical order—no use offending anyone! The "executor," or the one who was supposed to do something about the memo, was a lad named Bud Frump of the shipping department. His name was never actually included in the typed version, but was written in red pencil on the tenth carbon. See "Secondary Target," above.

From: Pierrepont Finch

Some authorities favor "Mr. Finch" in this position, but there is a certain disarming modesty and easy familiarity about plain "Pierrepont Finch." In fact, some of Finch's better-known memos were signed simply "Pont Finch."

SUBJECT: THE WICKET SITUATION

Never neglect a resounding title! This memo could have been titled "Put Plenty of Excelsior in Future Wicket Shipments," since that was the real, or secondary, purpose. A clod would have done so, but not Finch!

Few of us are aware of the alarming situation that confronts us with regard to our current wicket shipments.

This is good! It alerts the reader, puts him on his guard against real danger, and keeps him going through the meaty, or impressive passages. The sure-footed memowright knows the value of the word "alarming" in the first sentence. It is a particularly well-chosen word because it indicates that even though there is a real threat, you are on top of it.

I think first we should all be brought up to date on the background.

"Background," too, is good. All memos should have plenty of "background." It promises rich rewards for those who follow you through the ensuing paragraphs.

And because—though I hesitate to say it—the wicket background has become more or less inseparable from my own, I may have to sketch in a few personal details.

You are losing readers here, face it! But plunge on. This is the real treasure, or pay dirt, that you are bringing to your carefully chosen group of readers.

My intimate connection with the wicket situation dates back to its very inception.

At this point the memo becomes technical, and will be of small value to the lay or non-wicket reader. Suffice it to say that two or three closely written pages follow. One who threads his way through this treasure trove will discover that—lo!—Finch not only has a firm grasp on wickets, but on the entire industry as well. The branches are fairly groaning with such ripe fruit as this:

—Furthermore, my long research into the matter led me to the conclusion that—

And:

Though this is only my *personal* belief, it is one that few, at this stage, can dispute!

Perhaps the following anecdote will help to illustrate my point. Wander with me back through the years to the old Maple Street Plant.

For a page and a half one well-turned phrase follows another. The story, charming as it is, has little to do with the wicket situation. Its purpose is finer, higher, and broader. Rare indeed is the reader who does not emerge with the conviction that Finch is a capital fellow, stouthearted, clearheaded, brave, and reverent.

"Take your money," I said. "A Biggley boy I began and a Biggley boy I'll stay, damn you!"

After a few more scattered bon mots, Finch concludes thus:

There are a number of major steps that we can surely take in the future, but for the moment, aside from packing more excelsior in the wicket cases, we find ourselves in somewhat of a cul-de-sac. However, time will tell.

Small reason to remind the critical reader that this is true artistry, and in the Finch tradition. Finch has disposed of his real, or secondary, subject with a rapier thrust, piercing it concisely in one parenthetical phrase: "aside from packing more excelsior in the wicket cases." A fine example to follow!

(Signed)
Ponty

Though actually all copies—except the one to Bud Frump—had "Ponty" written in longhand at the end, the impression conveyed was that the *others* were signed "P.F." and that *only your own* was signed "Ponty," personally, in a spirit of brotherly affection. Finch's secretary had long since become expert at writing "Ponty" so that it was indistinguishable from the real thing.

9
BE AN IDEA MAN!

The very keystone of modern business is the Idea. In fact, no greater praise can be given you than to be called An Idea Man.

You may say, "But I've never had an idea in my life!" This may be true, but do not be discouraged! Men like you head many of our nation's greatest businesses.

They have learned that Idea Production is a little trick that can be mastered with very modest mental equipment. They have acquired it over the years, but you can pick it up in the few short seconds it takes to read this chapter.

There are several ways to produce ideas.

1. *Develop Them.* It is your function as a man who has both feet on the ground, to *develop* ideas. This means you will take the little worthless notions of others and add to each of them that important fillip that *makes it work*—and that makes the idea Your Own.

This requires Vision, but if you are made of the right stuff, you should have Vision to spare.

The undeveloped, worthless notions may come from any source. For example, one of your assistants may approach you:

> *"Uh, I've been working on this for some time, Mr. Finch."*
> *"Good spirit, son."*
> (Always encourage the little people.)
> *"Do you think I ought to write it out and send it along to J.B.?"*

"Let me be the judge of that, son. Just tell it to me in your own words."

If you decide the notion can be developed, be sympathetic and fatherly.

"Uh, do you think it will work, Mr. Finch?"
"No, no, not as it stands, of course not. Worthless. But it might be developed. Let me give it some thought, when I have time. Mighty good try, though. Good thinking!"
"Oh, thank you, sir!"

You will often find, then, that the notion needs very little of your magic touch to make it work. Put your stamp on it! Then, if you are successful, and if the management rewards you, *don't forget the little fellow* who started you on the notion. Send him a memo, a nice memo. He will cherish it. Don't be *too* specific, however. Sometimes the little people are ungrateful, and fail to realize the part you have played in putting the thing on the rails, in making it practical. Write something like:

"Your thoughts on the problem I was working on certainly helped. Thanks so much!"

2. *Call a Conference.* If you need something in a hurry, call in all your assistants, associates, or members of your department, if you have one. State the problem. Then tell them:

"Of course I've got the thing almost licked, but I wanted to get some of your thoughts on it. Just jot down your surface notions. Take all the time you want, as long as you have them on my desk by two."

(An arbitrary time limit is a good spur to thinking. Thinking—at least on *this* level—is best done under forced draft.)

Each little notion will no doubt be worthless, but by exercising your own Vision, you may be able to combine or develop them into something that will work, and something which, again, will be truly Your Own.

3. *Use Your Advertising Agency.* If you have kept your agency properly on its toes (see Chapter 15 on "How to Handle Your Advertising Agency"), you may find it of occasional help in producing ideas. Agencies employ people who do nothing but sit around and think up ideas. Use them!

Here again you will have to take their dreamy notions and Whip Them into Shape, stamp them with your own brand. The agency will not mind. In fact, the agency is used to it. They may even try to make you think that an idea that is wholly theirs is yours. Do not be deceived! Fiddle with it. It is your duty to improve everything.

4. *Use Your Subconscious.* When all else fails, you may have to use your own brain—for the original processes, that is.

Remember, your brain is like an iceberg. Only an insignificant part shows above the surface. The rest is submerged. This submerged part is your subconscious mind, and wise indeed is the businessman who makes his subconscious work for him.

Simply feed the facts to your subconscious and then relax. The more you relax, the better. Forget the problem. The answer will come to you. Sometimes it will come while you are shaving, or while you're sinking a putt. But it will come!

For example, let us say you have assembled a set of facts carefully, sparing no effort. Then as your high-caliber subconscious goes to work on them, strange things can happen.

> *"Oh, uh, Mr. Finch, you know all those figures and things I spent the last few nights getting up for you?"*
> *"Yes, son?"*
> *"Well, it just happened to occur to me that a solution might be simply to give the wickets a left-hand thread."*
> *"Amazing, isn't it! I knew it would come to me!"*
> *"Uh, beg pardon, sir?"*
> *"Ways of the subconscious are mighty strange, aren't they, son? Thanks for reminding me."*

You will have many other manifestations of the true power of your subconscious, able as it is to come to incredible solutions and even to implant them in other and lesser minds. It is difficult to explain this power to others, and many feel it is best not to try.

> *"It just came to me, Mr. Biggley. There I was, sitting in my office, and it just came to me."*
> *"Magnificent, Finch, really magnificent!"*

Make it clear, however, that the Idea Man is always working. You may not *look* as though you are working. To the untrained eye you may be drinking a Martini, or improving relations with the secretarial staff, but the big wheels are turning in your subconscious, the real work is going on in the great sunken iceberg of your mind, the source of your true power.

10

MAKE RESEARCH
WORK FOR YOU

[*Note: It should be pointed out here that there are two basic types of research, loosely classified as (1) white coat research and (2) blue suit research. The white coat, or laboratory type, will be handled for you by your advertising agency, which keeps a large stock of white coats in all sizes. We will be concerned here only with the second, or blue suit, type of research, largely involving public opinion, and including polls, market research, audience ratings, and the like.*]

Business used to be conducted, as our fathers would say, "by the seat of the pants," meaning actually that they just Used Their Heads.

This, of course, is no longer the case.

A man with a fine brain is mighty welcome in *any* business, as we have seen. His is the responsibility to make the basic decisions. However, if your mind is sometimes confused by the hurly-burly of the office, never fear. Business is happily not the willy-nilly, hit-or-miss affair it was in Dad's day.

Science has taken a firm hold. No matter how little thought you have time to give anything, with research at the helm you cannot make a wrong decision.

Everything is now done by research.

Test Your Product!

Remember, it isn't what your product *is* or *does* that is important. It's *what people think about it* that counts! Find this out! There are many companies that do nothing but ask people what they think. Use them!

Whatever you make, test it! Test the shape of your automobile, the flavor of your toothpaste, or the plot of your movie. You can be sure that *somebody* will buy tomorrow what a tested majority wanted yesterday.

Leave old-fashioned pioneering to others!

Make Science Work for You

The fainthearted will stop here, but not the rising young man. You will soon learn that this new science can be made to work for *you*. Many brilliant young fellows have risen rapidly to the top by remembering this cardinal principle:

> *The Primary Use of Research Is to Prove Your Point.*

After a poll has been taken, it is well to be on the side of the majority figures, but if you are caught with your percentages down, do not be discouraged.

Remember these simple handy ways to keep Science on YOUR side.

1. *Carry a Slide Rule!* The truly scientific businessman feels *naked* without his slide rule.

"Well, the latest Nielsen survey makes your recommenda-tion look pretty bad, eh, Finch?"

"It would look that way on the surface, wouldn't it," you counter, *slipping your bamboo and old ivory slide rule out of its saddle-stitched case and toying with it.*

"After all, ten percent favor your model and ninety percent favor mine."

"Entirely a surface reaction. Have you analyzed the 'Don't Knows' and 'No Opinions'?"

"Well, I, uh—"

"Reverses the trend entirely! Let me give you a sample." Turn to your slide rule, slide it about feverishly for several minutes.

"Mmmmmmmmm," you say, *"yes, that's right. Thirty-two point seven. You see?"*

"Thirty-two point seven of what?"

"It's the correlation. No child could miss it. Here, work it out for yourself!" Hand him the slide rule. If he can't work it he's done for and he knows it.

2. *Know the Language.* If you are caught in a statistical cul-de-sac, keep your head. Remember that facts and figures are putty in the hands of a man who really knows the language.

Memorize these simple phrases:

a. You may not see it in the *figures,* but the *trend* is obvious!
b. There's every reason to believe that the "Don't Cares" are with us.

   c. Of course it isn't an adequate sample.

   d. Forget the *figures*—look at the *curve!*

   e. Completely superficial! A depth interview would give an entirely different picture!

Or, if the results are disastrous:

   f. We've begun to question the validity of their whole method!

3. *Use Charts.* A good man with a bar chart can prove any point on either side of most arguments, but the true virtuoso prefers curves, either rising or falling.

> *"But the thing shows a dip!" your opponent may charge.*
> *"Ah," you counter, "but it's a healthy dip!"*

Many a rising young man has proved his point by using graphs sideways, or upside down. After all, it's the *spirit* that counts.

Maintain a scientific attitude, and keep your graph paper dry!

4. *Subscribe to ALL the Services.* Luckily there are dozens of companies that conduct these surveys. If one set of figures doesn't prove your point there is usually another that will.

> *"But, Finch, the Hooper shows conclusively that you're wrong!"*
> *"The Hooper! Oh, really!"*

"But you were quoting the Hooper last week!"

"It was perfectly valid *there! On this thing, Pulse has the only acceptable method. Simply read the questionnaires!"*

(It is always safe to assume that he hasn't.)

Observe these rules and you will soon discover what a powerful force public opinion can be—especially when it is working for *you.*

11
HOW TO MAKE MORE MONEY

Why Make More Money?

It is an easy thing, as this chapter will show, to double or triple your income.

But the question asked by so many is—*"Why?"*

You may be living a simple, happy life and not want to take on the extra cares, duties, and responsibilities that go with money. This is not a proper attitude.

True, there was a time when money meant dull, time-consuming meetings with investment men, visits to stuffy safe-deposit vaults, sleepless nights, and scheming women.

For the salaried man this is happily no longer the case!

Today you need never see the money at all. It will pass painlessly from your bank to your tax accountant and from him to the government, which will make good use of it dredging rivers, supporting farmers, printing pamphlets, and other useful works. The government will not bother or worry you about how it spends your money. It will be entirely out of your hands.

You may still ask, then, "Why make money?" as so many have. The answer is clear and ringing: *It is the American thing to do!*

Remember: Money is the only true indication that you have Made Your Mark. The man in the street, even your own office personnel, will not know how much you make, but if you are In the Money it will be stamped on you, it will be a badge of honor.

The difference between the $20,000-a-year man and the $40,000-a-year man is the difference between day and night, even though their take-home pay will differ negligibly. The higher-paid man will have prettier secretaries, more windows in his office, hand-blocked draperies, and a look of authority. His voice will carry weight wherever he goes.

There are two basic ways to make more money:

(1) by getting a raise at your own company, and (2) by leaving to join another company.

How to Get a Raise

Always remember that the first raises are the hardest. It is much harder to rise from $50 to $60 a week than it is, later on, to move from $10,000 to $15,000 a year.

This is because on a $50-a-week level you are an "employee," and therefore a natural enemy of management, whereas on the $10,000 and higher levels you are "one of us." The sooner you create the "one of us" attitude the better.

Here are some good devices, which should be used in rotation:

1. *Abject Poverty Device.* Do not overdo this! Be restrained, be brave.

> *"I don't mind, really sir. They say you think better on an empty stomach. It's just the children."*

Patches on the clothes should be made to look as though *you tried to make them match.*

Bring your lunch to the office, just a tired, worried sandwich—but do *not* complain about it.

> *"Oh, no, really, I prefer it. Frightful crowds in the restaurants. Nothing like a good, homemade sandwich."*

Remember your car, too:

> *"Sorry I'm late, sir. The poor old car keeps breaking down. I'll pick up some picture wire on the way home."*
> *"Picture wire?"*
> *"Yes, should fix it up fine. Keep the doors from falling off again."*

2. *The Philosophical Approach.* Pretend it isn't really the money you're after. This will put the whole thing on a higher plane.

> *"It just came over me, sir. What are we really* living *for? Both of us, I mean. Essentially we want escape. Feel the soil between our toes. Money's only a small part of it, really."*

He will be apologetic about giving you more money. He will know he can't put soil between your toes.

3. *The Simulated Job Hunt.* Never, of course, say you are looking for another job. Be mysterious. But always take a briefcase with you to lunch, and be seen leaving with it. You may fill it with sandwiches, laundry, rocks, or old memos, but it

must be *full.* An occasional sortie in midmorning or midafternoon is helpful, too.

How to Get a Better Job

Many have succeeded by hard work, lingering month after month at the same company, rising slowly through the ranks. They will reap a lasting reward.

However, you may be the brilliant, volatile type, unwilling to stay penned long to one desk or one job. Have no fear!

Be a Leapfrog. The truly expert leapfrogger advances even more rapidly than his stay-at-home colleague. And he is constantly in new surroundings, making new friends!

Stay one jump ahead. The skilled leapfrogger is never fired. True, you may often find (as most leapfroggers do) that you are *too good* for the job. You may sense this immediately, but your employer—whose brain may not be so keen—will probably take six months or so to discover it. Keep ahead of him. Jump! This will look better on your record, if a potential employer checks back on you:

> *"Uh, this fellow Finch, claims he worked for you five months in 1950. You fire him?"*
>
> *"No, can't say we did. He resigned. Said he had a better offer."*

Never SEEM to Leapfrog. No employer will want to hire you for six months. He may ask:

"Your record would indicate you've had twelve jobs in the last six years. How do you explain that?"

"They won't let *me settle down. Always getting better of-fers. Actually I've never been fired. You can check on that!"* (He will.) *"I'm looking for a spot now where I can really set-tle down and grow!"*

Sell Yourself. The true leapfrogger is a super self-salesman. Brilliant, confident, self-assured, with the first names of everyone in the industry at the tip of his tongue, he can dazzle any interviewer! Promise anything! You know you can deliver, but before you can really *prove* it you will be on your way to greener pastures.

How to Ask for Money

Your future employer will always ask how much money you expect to make. Do not be greedy. Your object is to serve. The money is only secondary. Make this clear.

However, it is well to remember a few handy hints:

1. *Never Ask for Money by the Week.* Never even mention money by the week. This is for clerks. Discuss it only *by the year,* and in thousands, casually, as "ten," "twenty," "fifty," or whatever you feel the traffic will bear.

2. *Never Be Apologetic.* Never say, "Would $4,500 be too much?" Say, instead, if asked:

"Now, about money, Mr. Finch—"

"Oh, money! *Hadn't thought much about it, frankly. Anything at all. Whatever you say. My place is pretty well organized, and I can always rent Southampton, temporarily. I could let things* slide *for a while on fifteen or twenty. Then when I prove to you I'm really worth* money *we can re-open it."*

Samples of Your Work

There are companies in which you may be expected to do some kind of useful work, or at least to have some special knack. These include publishers, motion-picture companies, radio or television broadcasters, photographers, art studios, and the like.

There are others, like advertising agencies, which in spite of feverish activity don't require any really *useful* work, but do need certain rudimentary skills.

For such companies you may be expected to write, paint, use a camera, or otherwise have some superficial cleverness.

As indicated above, it is well to avoid jobs like these. As a brilliant young man you will do best to concern yourself with Overall Operation and Formulating of Policy. This is easier work, requires no special talents or long dreary training, and is far more highly rewarded.

However, some people must do these things, and if you must be one of them you will have to show samples of your work.

Samples should be chosen carefully. In an advertising agency, for example, you will find large filing cases full of proofs. Don't be hasty! These are to represent *your* work, and it is always well to read them thoroughly before selecting. A pretty picture isn't everything. (Or, if you're an artist or layout man, don't be misled by a catchy phrase.) Choose some small black-and-white ads, too, along with the big four-color ones.

If you have actually written an acceptable one yourself, by all means include it. False modesty may be damaging.

Some authorities feel it is necessary to know who really *did* write (or lay out, or photograph, or draw) the sample. This is unnecessary. Just be sure your prospective interviewer didn't do it himself. People *do* move from job to job, you know. If so, the two of you will have a good laugh, but he may not hire you.

Disarm the Interviewer.

> *"Mmmmmm. You write this copy, too?"*
> *"No."*
> (He will look up, startled.)
> *"No?"*
> *"Not every word. I can't claim that. Client, you know. Kept changing this word back and forth."*

Once you have obtained a better job, repeat the whole process. But don't rush. Allow yourself several months to learn the business and to make lasting friends.

And of course there is always the chance to fall into something both permanent and tempting, as we shall see in later chapters.

12
HOW TO KEEP MONEY

By now we have surely made it clear that the real pleasure in money is simply *making* it, for its own sake. Our warnings against *keeping* money have been loud and firm.

However, there are still a few magnanimous souls who are willing to undergo this sacrifice and assume this responsibility.

Such a thing, as we have pointed out, is impossible for the salaried man except under special conditions.

"Should I Keep a Collector?"

This is a question asked by so many, and one that bears close examination. After all, one of the joys of having money is sharing it with others. Some prefer to give it directly to the *government as a whole,* which uses it, as we have pointed out, to improve the lot of people everywhere.

Others, feeling that this is impersonal at best, prefer giving money directly to *individual* members of the government, often to those same members of the Department of Internal Revenue who receive the other and more general gifts. These men, who are pitifully underpaid for the work they do, need far less of your money than the government as a whole, since they have fewer world-wide obligations.

They spend the money on simple, everyday pleasures, on their wives and children, and always seem to get good use out of it. It is heartwarming, too, to see their smiles of gratitude, so rarely given to those who simply send their checks to the general fund.

Thus it is with a heavy heart that the author feels impelled to advise against this practice. Though many do it, no doubt in a spirit of simple generosity, it is against the law. Unfair as such arbitrary rules may seem to you, they are the laws of the land and must be obeyed by us all.

Give Us Liberty!

However, there are increasing numbers of businessmen who, because of carelessness or foolish mistakes, often find themselves behind bars.

Unfortunate as this is, it is gratifying to note that the old social prejudices are rapidly approaching the vanishing point.

A short stay with the government is being accepted more and more as "part of the game," and some of our girls are devoting their afternoons to preparing going-away baskets, organizing visiting teams, and writing cheer-up letters.

Though it is true that you may form many valuable and lasting friendships among your fellow inmates, it should be pointed out that it is difficult not only to do your job from these institutions, but also to rise in your own organization. Many a man has been passed over for promotion because he was temporarily not "on the spot."

Hail to the Graduated Tax

Though breaking the law may be considered fashionable by some, it is not always necessary. In this country we have what is known as the "graduated income tax." This means, simply, that when you graduate to the really *big* money, a grateful government finds many little ways to let you keep it.

The very poor and the very rich pay relatively few taxes. It is the middle-income salaried man who supports the government. If you insist on keeping money, it is well to leave this classification as soon as possible and get into what is sometimes called the "real gravy."

Make It a Capital Gain

The capital gains law is a fine and generous system for encouraging initiative, free enterprise, and hard work.

It operates very simply. Let us say you are the world's greatest arm wrestler, able to command a million dollars a year in personal-appearance fees. If you just take the million you will have to pay more than ninety cents on the dollar in income taxes, and will keep less than $100,000, small return for your effort!

Take advantage of the capital gains law and it will be a far different story. Make a deal with, say, a rising canner of concentrated papaya juice. Buy 100,000 shares of stock at ten cents a share. Appear on his television program and in all his advertising. Soon the papaya juice will be so popular you can sell your stock at ten dollars a share, giving you a profit of $990,000, a capital gain, and taxable at about 25 percent. Thus you will clear more than $700,000, which will enable you to live as a good arm wrestler should.

Under this clever system arm wrestlers are encouraged to think about papaya juice as well as arm wrestling, more capital is poured into industry, and everyone benefits.

This method can be used on a more complicated but equally effective scale in most businesses.

> *"Somebody has to make the gears for the wicket sprockets, J.B., why not you and me?"*
>
> *"You and me, Finch?"*
>
> *"We start a company with our own fifty thousand or so, build it by giving it Biggley Company sub-contracts, and run it to a million-dollar corporation. Then we sell for a capital gain."*
>
> *"By gad, Finch, by gad!"*
>
> *"I'll do the organizing in return for stock, sir. Have some good men picked out already for the detailed work."*

Have an Expense Account

The expense account will be a powerful ally in your struggle to keep some of your own money. All business expenses are deductible, no matter how frivolous they may seem to you, as long as they are kept on a high plane. For example, your shipping clerk will be sternly reprimanded—and rightly so!—if he attempts to deduct his commutation fare from Mineola to the office, whereas a sympathetic government wisely allows you to deduct the expense of a few weeks in Miami, as long as you can show that it helped to further customer relations or improve business.

Many useful services are deductible if properly explained.

> *"Uh, Mr. Finch, how do you explain this deduction of $150 a week to a Miss Yvonne Schultz at 470 Park Avenue?"*
> *"Research, market research. She does it for me on a personal basis. Frightfully efficient girl, earns every penny."*

Remember that the government wants only its legitimate tax dollar. You will be encouraged to make all legal deductions.

Buy an Oil Well

You don't have to be from Texas to have unlimited and practically untaxable wealth. Anyone who can afford an oil well can do it. No need to pay most of your income in taxes. The lucky oil well owner can deduct most of his as "depletion of reserves."

A few sly fellows have tried to claim that by working they were depleting their own mental and physical reserves. A vigilant government soon put a stop to that. The law is intended to encourage investment and conserve mineral resources.

Anyone can imagine how morally dangerous it would be to try to conserve human resources.

13

HOW TO PLAY
COMPANY POLITICS

I t goes without saying that you, as a rising young man, will live a clean life, rise early, work hard, and keep your employer's interests at heart.

These are all laudable traits, but of course they will get you nowhere without a thorough understanding of company politics.

Company politics should never be confused with national politics or political parties, though it is safe to assume that if you expect to rise rapidly to the top you will either *be* a Republican or *seem* to be one.

Be a Politician

Do not confuse this with being a politician in the ward politics sense. Businesses are governed, not by the majority, but by the men at the top, in a manner reminiscent of the medieval Italian city-state. Read Machiavelli—and then learn the following easy rules:

1. *Pick the Right Team.* In your company, as in all healthy, live-wire groups, there are bound to be areas of friction. Enter them with a will.

There are always two or more factions fighting for control, or for favor with the Big Wheels. It is essential to maintain strict neutrality long enough to determine which side is going to win.

No matter how well you do your work, if you choose the wrong side you will soon be in a sorry plight indeed.

2. *Be a Pussyfooter.* During this wait-and-see period others may try to force you to choose sides. Resist them!

For example, during a heated argument at a meeting you may be asked:

"Well, Finch, what do you think about it?"

The chips would seem to be plainly down, but a skillful pussyfooter need not be dismayed.

"Oh, it's obvious, sir!" (Never seem to pussyfoot!) *"Mr. Blank's statement is so clear—"* (A smile here to Blank, who may still be in the running.) *"—that I would say by all means buy more wickets! On the other hand, Mr. Threep's point is certainly well taken!"* (Threep is far from being counted out, and you know his mother-in-law holds a big batch of stock.) *"I'd say buy sump pumps, too!"*

In short, steer a bold path, right down the middle. After the meeting it is well to see both Blank and Threep, separately.

"Hope I didn't let you down, sir. Hated to hurt poor old Threep's (Blank's) feelings. Wouldn't want to kick a man who's going down!"

3. *Make Your Move.* After it is clear that Threep, say, *is* going down, the humane thing to do is to finish him off as quickly as possible. Attack him freely, and preferably in Blank's presence.

"Threep's point is well taken," you say, with a condescending smile, *"if we assume his information is correct. However, it looks to me as though he has been badly misguided."* (You pity the poor old devil, discredit his whole team, yet maintain an attitude of great magnanimity.) *"In line with Mr. Blank's figures, it would be disastrous to follow Threep's recommendations. Buy wickets, buy more wickets, and drop the whole sump pump line!"*

If you administer the coup de grâce to Threep, Blank will soon make you his right-hand man. You are on your way up— well-deserved reward for courage and clear thinking.

From this point on, follow Blank loyally. There is nothing like loyalty, as long as your man moves up fast enough to leave plenty of room behind.

If he does not, never fear. You must think first of the company's good, and if Blank is not Doing His Job, you must not let sentiment interfere. By this time you should be skillful at giving people the business. Give it to Blank, in a nice way, and afterwards do your best to find him another job. He will thank you for it. Care for your friends, and they will care for you.

4. *Stab the Right Backs.* Your manner at all times should be friendly, kind, and courteous. The good businessman is everyone's Pal.

But from time to time some selfish person will stand in your way.

Before dispatching him it is well to ask yourself: Is he married to the boss's daughter? Is he a fair-haired boy? Is he related to a customer or client?

If he has attained his position because of ability, a few disparaging remarks *in the right ears* will do for him quickly—but beware the man who has deeper roots!

5. *Guard Your Own Back.* You can assume that your assistants will serve you loyally and selflessly, as long as you keep your distance.

But the wise businessman always protects his rear. The surest way of doing this is to be careful in choosing assistants. It can be done in several different ways. Let us examine them all.

    a. *The Happy-Moron Theory.* Your safest course is to hire only imbeciles as assistants. They will worship you—as assistants should!—and will never be able to threaten your position. If you are a good talker you should be able to convince management that they are doing a grand job, but only because they have you for guidance.

    b. *The Divide-and-Conquer Theory.* This is no course for timid souls. Hire the best men—but make them compete for your favor. You will find it an easy task to poison their little minds and turn them against each other—but in a constructive way. Make sure you are always the Great White Father to whom they will run in peril.

    c. *The Ugly-Duckling Theory.* One chap with extremely modest ability and a glib tongue rose rapidly to the top by this method. He hired brilliant but unpresentable assistants, men with fine minds but repulsive personalities who sat behind filing cabinets doing superb work for which he took full credit.

Few would have had the courage to take so daring a step!

But you may find a fourth and even better way. At this moment experiments are going on in offices throughout our nation.

6. *Upward and Onward.* Clearly the best way, however, to keep ahead of your assistants is to blaze a bold, straight path—forward! As you move rapidly ahead with giant strides, your assistants will have enough to do filling the posts you leave behind. You will be an inspiration to those under you. It is only those ahead who need beware!

7. *Choose the Right Wife.* Remember, the American home is sacred, and it is a shoddy fellow indeed who uses his wife to further his own selfish ends.

However, if you live in a small city or company town it is well to choose your wife carefully, as she, too, will have to play her part. Otherwise you may be forced to replace her, and this should *not* be done frequently, and then *only between jobs.*

Choose a wife who is adaptable and flexible, who will fit in well with the group. She should not, of course, have any definite opinions or any special mentality, as these will soon rub others the wrong way. It is important above all not to offend.

A college education is of great value to the company wife as long as she is careful not to let it creep into her conversation or influence her reading. The social graces, skill at cards, and ability to dress well, all these real tangible attributes of the college graduate, will stand her in good stead.

Most important is to find a girl whom the influential wives will admire. She must be a good clean-cut American girl, ready to make many sacrifices to endear herself to the women around her.

She must be prepared to perform a few simple services:

> *"Couldn't we pick up your little dears in the morning? After all, I'm used to getting up at six!"*

Or:

> *"I'm so glad you admire Hilda's cooking. Ponty was wondering if you wouldn't like to have her."*

And remember, soon the shoe will be on the other foot. As you rise in prestige and authority she will have *her* innings—if you're still willing to put up with her.

8. *Pick the Right Suburb.* If your job is in a very large metropolitan area, it is most important to choose the right suburb.

Remember, it is almost as easy to go from New York to Chicago as it is to go from Upper Hohokus, New Jersey, to East Squaque, Long Island. This is an advantage. Use it! It will insulate you from those who might annoy you, and put you right into the laps of those with whom you would like to be cozy.

Beware the Commuter's Bridge Game. It is a rare man indeed who remains long on speaking terms with his "cronies" of the morning and evening bridge game. If you *must* play bridge, choose men in another company, preferably another industry. Some men are slow to forgive, and smoldering hatreds have blasted many a budding career.

Be a Nodder. The skillful Paper Reader (as opposed to the Bridge Commuter) soon learns to give influential acquaintances a warm, charming nod-and-smile as he passes their half-empty seats and sits *with a total stranger.*

This is to be recommended even if the acquaintance is important to you in company politics. It may seem a wasted opportunity, but it may prevent your being transferred abruptly to North Dakota.

9. *Pick the Right Country Club.* This, of course, is a *must.* The gay man-to-man gemütlichkeit of the locker room, the rough-and-ready camaraderie of sand trap and water hole will stand you in good stead in the hurly-burly of the business world.

One keen young man made a smashing success by always managing to arrive first at his boss's ball when it lay in the rough. After deftly kicking it out of a rabbit hole he would say:

> *"Here it is, J.B., in the clear!"*
> *"Good boy, Finch. Mighty lucky I'm not in that damned rabbit hole!"*

"Yes, sir, mighty lucky!"

"Matter of fact, I always seem to have better luck when I go around with you, Finch!"

But this, as we will see, goes almost beyond the level of Company Politics—and approaches a higher one. We will take it up in our next chapter.

14

HOW TO BE A
FAIR-HAIRED BOY

Over and above the hurly-burly of office politics there is a Higher Level. This is known as playing directly to the Old Man, or getting to be a Fair-Haired Boy.

The most direct way, of course, is through the Old Man's daughter, but if he doesn't have one, if someone else has beat you to her, or if on seeing her you feel it's too high a price to pay, keep your chin up.

There are many other ways to make yourself known and loved.

Remember, there may be a human side to the Old Man.

The Hobby. Rare indeed is the successful businessman who does not have some little corner of life that he holds dear. Discover what it is, and join him in it! If the Old Man raises hamsters, collects cigar bands, or plays the zither, your course is clear.

Once you have done some preliminary research you may fire your opening gun, say, in the elevator.

> *"Got to hurry home, sir. The little devils are whelping."*
> *"Whelping, Finch? Don't tell me you're a mongoose man!"*
> *"Are you, too, sir? We are a rare breed, aren't we? Tell me, do you favor snake meat or kippers?"*

You will be asked to his place before long. After this it is only a matter of time.

If you live in the New York area it is not strictly necessary to mess with the little beasts. A handy reference book will supply you with plenty of conversation.

In a smaller town you may actually have to build a rig or pen or whelping stand, because he may want to come over to your place "to see the little devils" or "to try my hand with your shuttlecock."

Only in rare cases will there be any mental effort. You will find that the Old Man has simple pleasures, the major share of his intellect having been used to get him where he is.

You may profit by his example. Intellectual pursuits will give you small reward!

One word of caution: Do not follow the Old Man willy-nilly into *all* hobbies. If his interest lies in helping and encouraging young ladies, leave him to his own devices. He will not want your companionship.

In this case you will have to find another approach. There are many, as we will see.

The Old School Tie. You are fortunate indeed if the Old Man is a loyal alumnus. If he happens to come from some particularly vile backwater college—and has an inferiority complex about it—you have indeed struck a rich vein.

A few days spent at Old Ivy State Teachers Normal will supply you with all the necessary information and equipment. You need not bother with scholastic history or activities. Leave that to the professors. It will be enough to memorize the scores of all football games back to, say, 1903, the names of all local saloons, fraternities, dance halls, and traditional pranks, rushes, proms, and interclass wars. If your research indicates the Old Man excelled at the Hop, Skip, and Jump, or arm wrestling, bone up on that, too.

The local pawnshop will supply you with school rings, ties, pins, pennants, and old footballs painted with historic scores.

Once equipped, the rest is simple. A good opening wedge may offer itself on a Monday following Old Ivy's disastrous defeat by a traditional rival. Shun obvious signs of mourning. But manage somehow to get close to the Old Man and mutter:

"Sorry, sir. Not myself today. Rarely touch a drop, but I did belt off one strong one yesterday. Those damned Chipmunks!"

"Chipmunks?" (His nostrils will begin to quiver.)

"Oh, beg pardon, sir, you can't be expected to know. The old school took quite a drubbing Saturday. Old Ivy."

"Old Ivy? You're not an Old Ivy man, uh—"

"Finch, sir. Old Ivy, '24."

"Well, by God, Finch! Old Ivy, by God! Well, we'll get the damned Chipmunks next year, won't we?"

"We did it in '27 and we'll do it again, sir, if we ever get Ozymanowsky off the sick list!"

If you play your cards right, anything can happen, perhaps even:

"Oh, uh, Finch, I'm driving up to Old Ivy this Saturday. Like to come along?"

"Oh, would I, sir! Wouldn't miss that Framingham Teach-ers battle for anything!"

Once at Old Ivy, be bold! Wear your class numerals promi-nently. No need to worry that you'll be exposed. Feel safe in rushing up to the first '24 that you see:

"Well, well, Bampton! Good old Bampton!"
"Uh, I'm Gillingham, Bill Gillingham."
"Bill, of course! Sorry!"
"Great to see you again, uh—"
"Finch, Ponty Finch."
"Oh, sure, Finch. Had it on the tip of my tongue."
"Never forget those nights we spent down at the old greasy spoon, huh?"
"Those were the days, huh, Finch?"

You will soon be one of the boys. And you may soon be Spe-cial Assistant to the President, too.

The Lowly Beginning. If the Old Man is one of that rugged but vanishing breed who Started at the Bottom, play your cards far differently.

Go into the factory and find some of the old workmen who started at the bottom with him and are, more or less, still there.

"Yup, Mr. Finch, I still remember when young Johnny— we called him Johnny, then—started at the old plant down

on Maple Street. Pot-walloper. Only nine years old. Bright boy, though. Used to steal our lunches. Yup!"

Take your time. Soak up plenty of Old Plant lore. Then make a bold move. Head straight for the Old Man's office:

> *"We're taking up a collection for Old Grommick, sir."*
> *"Oh? Not dead is he?"*
> *"The bends, sir. I'm just collecting from us old-timers."*
> *"Good Old Grommick!"*
> *"Yes, sir, grand old man! Taught me all I ever knew about pot-walloping. I was just a kid. Fourteen. Down at the old Maple Street plant."*
> *"Oh? Started down there, too, did you, uh—"*
> *"Finch, sir. No substitute for the School of Hard Knocks, ain't that right, sir?"* (Note: An occasional "Ain't" or "He don't" is valuable in this approach, even if you're a cum laude from Harvard.)
> *"Damn' few men see that these days, Finch! Lot of damned mollycoddles!"*

A few short months of this and you'll be a marked man.

The Old Hometown. It is equally effective to adopt the Old Man's hometown. Proceed in a similar manner. Any good student should be able to ring the necessary changes.

Multiple Fair-Hairism

The keener students among you may well pose this question:

"What if we're not sure who the Old Man is?"

If this query is on *your* lips, too, tread carefully. The scrap heap is filled with well-meaning lads who have polished the wrong apples. Make sure! Look before you leap!

Choose the Right Man. If you have an opportunity to see him in action you need have few doubts. Use this simple "No" test! Many can say no to some of the people some of the time, but only the Old Man can say no to all of the people all of the time.

The Double-Barreled Situation. Pity the poor lad who serves two or more Old Men! If *your* company is a biumvirate, or even a triumvirate, play your cards carefully, for yours is a dangerous game. You have several courses of action:

1. *Place Your Bet.* Pick the winner. This is daring, and recommended only to the devil-may-care lad with private income.

2. *Wait.* It probably won't last long. Whenever there are two or more Old Men they will be locked in mortal combat. All but one are sure to go.

3. *Be a Multiple Fair-Haired Boy.* If you are made of the right stuff you will choose this course. Dangerous, yes, but a good man can bring it off.

Narrow the Field. Remember, you cannot be loved by everyone, no matter how lovable you may be. It is unsafe for the average student to play more than two horses, so to speak, at once, though there are cases on record of successful three- or even four-pronged fair-hairism.

Do Not Mix Your Approaches. Remember, the wise young man has only one school, one hometown, and one hobby. The careless lad may fall, for example, into the Pitfall of the Multiple Old School Tie:

> *"Good boy, that Finch! We build the right stuff up at Old Ivy!"*
> *"Old Ivy? But, J.B., Finch is an Aggie! Went up with me for the arm wrestling!"*

Few can climb out of such a hole. In fact, the only shafts you will have left in your quiver will be a disarming frankness or a pretty confusion.

Beware, too, the Curse of the Multiple Hobby:

> *"Steady nerves, that boy Finch! Nothing like a night at the whelping stand to bring out your true colors!"*
> *"Whelping stand? But Finch is helping me cross-pollinate! Up to his hips in paper bags! Has been since the equinox!"*

Suffice it to say, then, that the pitfalls of fair-hairism, either single or multiple, are many—but the lad who brings it off is well on his way to the highest levels.

15

HOW TO HANDLE YOUR ADVERTISING AGENCY

Most businesses must advertise, and therefore—whether you like it or not!—you may be forced at one time or another to come in contact with an advertising agency.

You have only to read current fiction to know that all agencies are made up of people of low moral fiber. They would naturally drift into this business with its promises of quick, easy money, its tinseled glamour, and its appeal to the primitive human instincts.

Be on your guard!

Beware of "Creative" People

Advertising agencies are forced to hire so-called creative people. They are artists, writers, musicians, radio and television directors, and the like.

They are sure to give you trouble.

It may *look* as though they are thinking about your problem, but they are not. The writers are thinking about the books they plan to write exposing advertising (and probably *you*); the artists are wondering if they could earn a living making batiks or painting sweet peas on teacups; and the musicians are mentally inserting you into a tone poem as a discordant squeal.

You will find it difficult even to speak their language.

The agency has tried to make it easy for you by keeping you away from these people. It has provided keepers or overseers called Account Executives. They are hired for their rugged good looks, their flair for wearing clothes, and their skill—

sometimes brutal but always effective—in handling creative people.

They know exactly how far an artist or writer will bend without breaking.

Make them your friends! Profit by their experience! They will be "your kind of people."

Fight Fire with Fire. If worse should come to worst, however, and you are forced into direct contact with "creative" people, it is best to fight fire with fire.

Use their own weapons against them. Some useful devices are: the falsetto scream, the threat of suicide, the threat of taking away their pencils or colored crayons, and the tantrum.

The tantrum, when used to combat the "creative tantrum," is usually termed a counter-tantrum.

Copy Writing Is Easy

The agency will try to make you believe that the preparation of advertising copy is a mysterious and artistic process. In fact, among the writers of magazine advertisements you may find some old duffers who even think the *writing* itself is important. Do not be misled.

"This is for plain people, ain't it?"
"Yes, Mr. Finch."
"And I'm plain people, ain't I? Come in here, Miss Jones, and I'll dictate how this oughta read."

(Note the carefully studied "down-to-earth" language, so effective against fussy writers.)

Generally speaking, however, it is best not to get too close to the actual writing. The best way is to have the agency people spread the ads out on the floor. If the agency is on its toes, the layouts should cover a nine by twelve rug. Keep them on the floor, don't get too close to them. It's the overall impression that counts.

> *"Uh, I like that one."*
> *"The up and down one, Mr. Finch?"*
> *"No, that one on the end."*
> *"That's the brief case, Mr. Finch."*
> *"Simple, that's what, simple!"* (Never retreat!) *"Doesn't look so busy."*

Since copy writers are often lazy and slovenly, it is best never to show approval, and yet—this is important—never to tell them exactly what you want, which would be doing their work for them. Your attitude must always be one of deep and unsatisfied yearning. Some good phrases for use in this connection are:

> *"You oughta noodle this around some more."*
> *"It isn't punched up enough. What it needs is more* sock.*"*
> *"You oughta countersink the idea."*
> *"Oh, I like it, it just doesn't reach out and* grab *me."*
> *"Now this isn't copy, but—"*

Many men, by doing little more than repeating these magic phrases or simple variations of them, have risen rapidly to posts as advertising managers, and some have even been hired, at fantastic salaries, by the agencies themselves.

Be a Showman

As a businessman you are lucky indeed to be alive in this day and age. In father's time the man of commerce spent his dreary days in the drab round of buying and selling.

Not so today.

With the rise of television the businessman finds himself firmly in the saddle as America's Number One Showman, determining the entertainment for the masses, who are also his customers.

This is a great opportunity—and a big responsibility, too.

Don't Be a High-Brow. Leave fancy theater stuff and long-hair music to the highbrow newspaper critics. Your duty is to the masses.

Remember, there are a hundred real typical people for every highbrow.

Use the Bridge Test. Try this handy rule of thumb! If your wife can "get the point" *while playing bridge,* the show is okay. If not, don't spare the rod. Keep the entertainers pepped up. Call them up *first thing* the morning after the broadcast.

126

"Hello, hello, this is Mr. Finch!"

"Huh, whazzat?"

"Wake up, man! I've been up for hours! Got to get up early in this business!"

"Uh, yes, Mr. Finch!"

"Listen, you boys have gotta give this show a hypo!"

"Didn't you like it, Mr. Finch?"

"Stank! Wanta know what my wife said to me right after it was over?"

"What, Mr. Finch?"

"She said she didn't get it! She didn't get it, man, and part of the time she was dummy! Gave it her almost undivided attention. We want a whole new deal next week."

"Well, uh, next week's script is all written."

"Throw it out! What are we paying those writers for?"

Keep on pepping them up like this, and pretty soon you'll have the show whipped into shape. The show people may grumble, but they'll thank you in the end.

Be a Television Expert. It is your duty to lead the way, and you can only do this by being an expert. Be one!

You can accomplish this easily, as so many smart businessmen have before you, after a few hours of keen application.

You need not concern yourself with the technical, or gadgety, phase. There are lots of little men around to take care of *that*.

Just learn a few simple phrases like "dolly," "pan," "super," and "cut." You will find it is easy—and mighty satisfying, too—to throw them around, and work them into the conversation.

It is better not to know what these phrases mean. Use them freely. You will soon be regarded as a man to reckon with.

Know Your Public Relations

Only after you have hardened yourself with long exposure to advertising men should you enter the still blacker morass of public relations. Dignified as it sounds under this euphonious title, you will be dealing with publicity and with press agents.

These fellows, you will soon discover, are a breed of desperate, hard-drinking men, many of whom have been driven out of the more respectable fields of advertising and journalism by outraged colleagues, and—more often than not—by their own love of loose living. Some of them, it is true, are actually employed by advertising agencies, but are usually kept on separate floors, or are otherwise insulated from the regular employees.

Yet you will have to "play ball" with these men, may even have to maintain some personal contact with them, distasteful as this may be. They will be furnishing you with a valuable commodity—publicity—which is essentially advertising you don't have to pay for. That is, it is not paid for in a formal, well-regulated way, but rather on a basis of threats, bribery, and the use of strong drink and loose women.

The publicity man will claim that his stock-in-trade is Ideas, but it will soon be apparent where the real thinking comes from.

"Uh, Red, here's something the American people are really ready for."

"Yes, Mr. Finch."

"It's got a real news *value, this new double sprocket wicket of ours. Now my idea is, why not just get us a three- or four-page spread of pictures in* Life *on it, okay?"*

He has nothing left to do but have the pictures taken, fix up some little "angle," and get it in the magazine.

Some day you may even be called upon to make a personal sacrifice. After you have reached a position of true eminence, you yourself may be the subject of personal publicity. When such a time comes, remember to put aside your own feelings of modesty. The good of the company is at stake.

"Red, uh, this picture of me. I'm not thinking of it personally, but you know newspaper reproduction."

"We retouched it, Mr. Finch."

"Just thought this one might be a better likeness. May be ten, twelve years old, but you can see I haven't changed."

They will write personal "blurbs" about you, too. Watch these carefully. It will be your duty to see that they are modest, factual, and easy to read.

"I just changed this part, Red, where it says 'one of the men who originated the double sprocket wicket' to 'the man who.' Makes it read better, don't you think?"

You will find generally that the time you take with advertising and publicity men is well spent. Just remember that a gulf will always exist between their ways of life and yours. Keep it there. Maintain your own moral standards at all times, regardless of your associates.

16
SEX IN BUSINESS,
ITS USES AND ABUSES

There are many who argue that sex has no part in a book such as this, written largely for use in schools of business. This is a narrow point of view and one that will get little sympathy from the author.

To the businessman, his job and his company must be everything, and to them he must be prepared to dedicate himself without reservation. The man who holds back, who, for selfish reasons, fails to give *all* of himself, will soon be unmasked.

This duty you owe not only with your brain, but in many cases with your body as well.

Be a Ray of Sunshine

More often than not you will find that the Old Man has for a secretary an aging maiden who has been with him for thirty years. She will be battered, moist, harassed, and often called Jonesy.

It is safe to assume that if the Old Man ever had a romantic interest in her it has long since passed. He keeps her now because she is efficient and always remembers when it is time for his pills.

It will be your duty to bring sunshine into her life.

In fact, no sacrifice you can make for her is too great, though happily the Supreme Sacrifice is seldom necessary. It will usually be enough to buy a slightly wilted and almost pitiful handful of flowers from a street vendor. Take them to her with a boyish smile.

"*Uh, Jonesy, I know these aren't much, but—*"

"*How nice, Pierrepont!*"

"*They just seemed to match your eyes, and, well, they just cried out, 'These are for Jonesy!'*"

You will have brought sunshine into a drab life, and though you may not have intended to, you may have opened new doors to the Old Man.

"*Oh, Mr. Biggley, young Finch has been waiting so long to see you.*"

"*Finch, who's he?*"

"*He's that sweet boy from Old Ivy—the one that works so hard. He's a great admirer of yours, Mr. Biggley.*"

Others may try this approach, too. It is well to be on your guard.

"*If it weren't for you and Jimmy Watson, Pierrepont, I'd just go for days without flowers.*"

"*Nice fellow, Watson. Just can't figure his taste in women. What does he see in that redheaded kid in General Files—the one in the white sweaters?*"

Your rival may have a nasty surprise the next time he wants an audience!

"*Anyone else to see me, Jonesy?*"

"*The Watson boy was waiting awhile.*"

"Watson, Watson?"

"He's that rather brash boy with the smirk. Somehow I don't think he respects *you, Mr. Biggley. I told him you were very busy."*

Keep Posted

Your next personal sacrifice will come shortly later in your career. At this time you will have your own secretary and presumably your most dangerous rival will have one, too. It is your rival's secretary, working as she does in the gloomy shadow of an unpleasant man, who needs a comforting hand and a cheering word. Give it to her. She will appreciate it.

"Oh, Mr. Finch, you do the cutest *things!"*

"You're a pretty cute thing yourself! What was that you started to say about Watson's memo to Mr. Biggley?"

"It wasn't anything, really, only one paragraph about you. I'll get you a carbon of it tomorrow morning at the office."

Do not fear that your rival will try similar tactics, if you have selected either a beauty or a beast, as outlined in Chapter 5. The beast would require too great a sacrifice, and the beauty we can assume would have good reason for personal loyalty to your cause.

Be Generous

Soon you will have reached a position where you can adopt a completely selfless attitude. It will then be your duty to go about doing the best you can in your modest way to raise morale, to gain understanding of the employees' problems, and to make it clear that the management has a personal and deep-seated interest in the lowliest typist or file clerk.

Some men even go farther, seeing to it that suitable girls are brought in, ones that will profit best by a helping hand and a friendly word.

In scores of progressive companies this personal and intimate approach is showing good results, and in many cases has taken the place of the old Suggestion Box.

Remember the Woman's Angle

The forward-looking businessman must also be aware that women are playing an ever-increasing role in our economy. Few products are not bought primarily by women, and the executive who does not understand her point of view is courting disaster.

It is for this reason that many of today's business leaders range far afield, even beyond their own employees, into the myriad homes of America.

Their harvest is a rich one indeed. How often will their true purposes be misunderstood!

For none of these personal sacrifices can the businessman expect public recognition or open reward. Day by day, night by night he must go on, anonymous, selfless, unsung.

It would be well if all of us would doff our hats for a moment in tribute to those who have made their mute sacrifices. The annals of modern business would be full indeed if only their stories could be told.

17
BE A BIG BROTHER

And so you will climb the ladder of success, rung by painful rung, until you have reached the top. Then you, too, will be called the Old Man or some other rough-and-ready term of endearment.

Continue to look ahead. There will always be new horizons.

But remember, too, that it is now your duty to look back, to lend a helping hand to those who are following you along the road. It is your mission now to be a Big Brother.

Share Your Experience

It should be easy for you, remembering the hard knocks you received, to smooth the path, to lighten the load for those younger and perhaps weaker ones who follow.

Talk to them, as many of them as you can get together at once, and preferably where they will have an opportunity to hear you all the way through without having to leave.

The company dinner is a fine spot for such a talk! Weigh your words carefully, they will be remembered.

> "—and as I look upon your young, eager faces, I remember the day I started at Biggley and Finch, which was then, of course, just Biggley and Company. And I remember my watchword—Work—W-O-R-K—Work! Gentlemen, there is no shortcut to success, no substitute for hard work, for courage, for loyalty, and, men, for GUTS!"

You should be able to go on in this vein for some time, happy in the knowledge that you are building character with every word.

Save Them from Themselves

Great as your inspiration may be, there will be some who will try to take the shortcut, the easy way. It is your duty to save them from themselves, to set them upon the right path.

> *"It's young Bibber, Mr. Finch."*
> *"Who?"*
> *"Young Bibber, sir, that nice boy who says he's from Old Ivy."*
> *"Throw the little rotter out, Miss Jones!"*
> *"But Mr.—"*
> *"And throw out that mangy flower, too!"*

Let them realize that your personal friendship can never take the place of real honest sweat—or of clear, level thinking, either!

> *"Bibber, sir, Spruance Bibber! Just happened to hit on a promising idea. Bit daring, sir. How about putting more excelsior in the wicket shipments?"*
> *"Your own idea, Bibber?"*
> *"Oh, yes, sir."*
> *"Then let me remind you that we've been doing it ever since I wrote that memo on it in 1937!"*

Be tireless in your efforts to point their young eager noses in the right direction.

> *"Just wondered how you rated my old office, Bibber."*
> *"It's this code, Mr. Finch. Frideful draft in my ode place—"*
> *"We'll find you a nice warm spot, son. There's a cozy corner in back of the old mimeograph machine."*

Remember, as the twig is bent so the tree grows. Keep bending it!

> *"Oh, working this morning, Bibber?"*
> *"Gosh, is it morning already, Mr. Finch?"*
> *"Yes, and it just started to rain. Better take your umbrella into the hall. It's dripping on the carpet."*

You will have a happy glow indeed as you see the young twigs growing, the branches sprouting, and even the first fruit forming on the boughs. But you still cannot cease your encouragement, cannot withdraw your helping hand.

> *"Think I'll run out to the plant, Mr. Finch. Quality check."*
> *"Good, Bibber, good. I'll phone you there."*
> *"Well, uh, may be difficult to locate me, sir, I—"*
> *"Don't worry, son, you leave the trouble to us. We'll find you!"*

Dedicate Your Leisure Hours

The true Big Brother sacrifices not only the working day, but his leisure hours as well. Time-consuming as this may be, you will find that it often brings with it its own reward in opportunities for guidance and building of character. Surround yourself with members of your own Team, and fill your leisure hours to overflowing.

> *"You, too, Mr. Finch? Might have known to look at you that you were a compost-heap man!"*
>
> *"Great Scott, Bibber, it's a small world!"*
>
> *"Does something to me, sir. I can just stand there and watch it rot."*
>
> *"Maybe you'd like to drop around over the weekend and muck around with us."*
>
> *"Well, I'd, uh, I sure would, sir."*
>
> *"You'll have to do most of the* hard *work, boy, but you won't mind if your heart's in it."*

The exercise will do them a world of good, but don't feel obligated to push them ahead in the company. The pleasant hours in the healthful sun will be reward enough.

The eager young minds of these striplings will be quick to sense any crosscurrents in the organization. You may use them as wind indicators, as barometers. It will help you to realize that no man stands alone and that others may seek a place beside you.

"Good boy that young Bibber, eh, Watson?"

"Capital, Finch, capital! Mighty keen man with a tuning fork!"

"Tuning fork?"

"Regular whiz! Been tightening my strings for a fortnight!"

Even after you have nursed and guided the youngsters to posts of real responsibility, you still cannot rest. Your job as a Big Brother is never done.

"Well, now that you have poor Watson's four windows, Bibber, you should be mighty happy!"

"Indeed I am, Ponty. As I was saying to dear old Biggley—before they took him away—what a grand place to work!"

"Well, uh, Spruance, we try to keep Finch and Company a Happy Ship."

"All I ask is to be in your crew, Ponty."

"I'm sure you do, uh, Spruance. It's just that sometimes I see you staring at me rather strangely."

"Admiration, old boy, admiration. After all, I've patterned my life on yours. Matter of fact, Ponty, I was just thinking up a few simple words to say to the stockholders at the next meeting. Thought I'd take my text, so to speak, from the ring-ing words you spoke to me when I was scarcely a boy. 'Bibber,' you said, 'always remember this—it isn't so much whether you win or lose—but how you play the game!'"

Brave words, indeed, for us all to cherish. It is well for us to remember, too, that kindness and consideration play an ever-increasing role in our business lives.

"You're looking a bit peaked today, Spruance. Think you're due for a nice rest!"

"Well, Ponty, maybe a few weeks in—"

"Nonsense, son! I mean a real *rest! Happens we need a new manager at the old fiber chopping plant in Mississippi. Plenty of spare time to relax."*

"Damned decent of you, Ponty—but am I really qualified? Gromble *deserves* that job—*he's* earned *it!"*

"How like you, Spruance! No, boy, it's yours. Two or three years down there in the warm sun and you'll be a new man!"

Think of others—and they will think of you.

A Parting Word

And now, as we close this book, who among us will not feel a tingle of anticipation, an urge to follow the footprints that have been laid out so carefully—and stretching we all know where.

May all of us, profiting by this brave example, start out upon the highways and byways of business with new resolve, and with new courage.

ABOUT THE AUTHOR

Shepherd Mead's outrageous success is a result not of following the precepts of this book (though he knows thousands who have) but of his unique ability to do without sleep, a secret he bought from an East Indian fakir while cycling with rod and camera from ashram to ashram. (Mead was abroad, riding a bicycle and sowing dissension, for several months in 1936. The whole world knows what happened a short three years later.)

He has not slept since October 28, 1936, the date of his return from overseas, with the possible exception of one twenty-minute period in the spring of 1946 when he feels he "may have dozed off."

Known in the ad game as Sleepless Mead, he rose like a shot from the ranks of the mail boys to his present position of wealth and power. This was accomplished not through any particular intelligence or ability, but purely because he was awake at all times.

While others slept, Mead worked, or appeared to, which is much the same thing. For a while, in fact, it was believed that the building at 444 Madison Avenue was haunted, and that a ghost was pacing the halls between midnight and dawn, its head tucked underneath its arm. Investigation proved it was only Mead, drifting about the stairwells carrying the wax effigy of an account executive, pierced in several vital spots with thumbtacks and unbent paper clips.

Being a captain of industry and siring three children kept Mead occupied only twenty hours a day and he was forced to find something to do to keep from biting his nails. A friend suggested writing, to which he replied with a hoot of derision. However, he gave it a quick trial and found instant success; he took to gnawing on the space bar of an old Underwood, and his nails soon resumed their healthy growth.

A by-product was a number of typewritten pages which he bound as plays, and which were bought with careless abandon by countless Broadway producers. This led to Mead's fame as America's Best-Loved Unproduced Playwright. One season, in fact, he set a record (still unbroken!) by having eight plays not running on Broadway at the same time.

He turned effortlessly to the novel and soon proved master of that field, too. His last two published works—*The Magnificent MacInnes* and *Tessie, the Hound of Channel One*—were greeted with shouts of praise by the critics and bought by lending libraries everywhere.